EVERYTHING YOU KNOW ABOUT JOB HUNTING IS WRONG. THIS IS THE GUIDE TO HELP YOU GET IT RIGHT.

Your job hunt is at a dead end. You've answered dozens of ads, gone on just as many interviews, and you still don't have an offer.

In the age of corporate downsizing and changing hiring practices, you need more than a perfect résumé and batting a thousand on the questions that are fired at you. You need a new mindset. Independent consultant and corporate headhunter Nick Corcodilos has taught thousands of people how to take control of their job hunting by mastering "the new interview." Say goodbye to résumés, cover letters, sweaty palms, and stupid interview questions. Turn up your intelligence, your skills, and your expertise—that's what a successful manager is waiting to see.

"Like sports and warfare, interviews have no gray area. You either win the job or get left out in the cold. *Ask the Headhunter* is the ultimate battle plan for victory in the world's toughest game—landing the job of your dreams."   —Captain Bruce Ollstein, author of *Combat Golf*

"The most original, provocative job search guide I know. Any job aspirant looking to stand out from the herd—and any hiring manager hoping to get it right the next time around—should read this."   —Paul Cohen, author of *Working Wisdom: Timeless Skills & Vanguard Strategies for Learning Organizations*

NICK A. CORCODILOS, Director of North Bridge Group, has earned his credentials as a headhunter in the intensely competitive high-tech world of Silicon Valley. He has helped many managers, engineers, and other professionals obtain positions in companies such as Hewlett-Packard, GE, Xerox, IBM, Honeywell, and Bell Aerospace, and advised thousands of job hunters and employers on his popular *Ask the Headhunter* forum on America Online. He lives in Lebanon, New Jersey.

"An invaluable aid. The book guided me through the process and provided the advice and counsel for an effective interview which was successful in producing an offer I accepted."

—James A. Wick, manager, Intel

"A real eye-opener, should be a must read for everyone! Wish I had it twenty years ago! Good insight on what happens in the entire interviewing/hiring process."

—Mary Ann J. Boyle, senior vice president, Marriott International

"An iconoclastic, cut-to-the-chase point of view on how to find and win the right job. And if you're a manager, a new way to think about hiring." —*Electronic Engineering Times*

"*Ask the Headhunter* made a huge difference. . . . By preparing me to *do the job* rather than just the interview for it, you gave me the confidence I needed to present myself as the solution to the interviewer's business problem."

—Gerry Zagorski, business development manager, AT&T Wireless Services

"Forget everything you have ever learned about how to behave during a job interview. . . . This book is an unusual opportunity to learn from an expert." —*Princeton Packet Business Journal*

"I was involved in an interview process for a perfect situation that had bogged down over the wrong things. The advice to project *I'm here to do the work* was perfect. I left the manager in shock and had an offer within twelve hours for 10 percent more than I had expected."　　　　　　　　　　　　　　—Bruce Jones, Norell, Inc.

"Gives one an insight into the true method of looking into a company of choice."　　　　　　—Warren Davis, procurement manager, Pepsi Cola International

"*Ask the Headhunter* is guaranteed to change, for the better, the way you think about the whole job and career process. It is the best job search book in the world. It cleared my head of a lot of clutter about work and helped teach me to create my own job."
　　　　　　　　　　　—Anthony Bennie, president, PetReps, Inc.

"Wow! What an excellent book! *Ask the Headhunter* has opened my eyes wide. I sure knew the standard hiring procedures didn't work well, but now I'm learning why."
　　　　　　　　　　　　　　—John Doyle, WAGA-TV, Atlanta

Ask the
Headhunter

reinventing
the interview to
win the job

Nick A. Corcodilos

Foreword by Nancy K. Austin

A PLUME BOOK

PLUME
Published by the Penguin Group
Penguin Putnam Inc., 375 Hudson Street,
New York, New York 10014, U.S.A.
Penguin Books Ltd, 27 Wrights Lane, London W8 5TZ, England
Penguin Books Australia Ltd, Ringwood, Victoria, Australia
Penguin Books Canada Ltd, 10 Alcorn Avenue, Toronto, Ontario, Canada M4V 3B2
Penguin Books (N.Z.) Ltd, 182–190 Wairau Road, Auckland 10, New Zealand

Penguin Books Ltd, Registered Offices:
Harmondsworth, Middlesex, England

First published by Plume, an imprint of Dutton Signet,
a member of Penguin Putnam Inc.

First Printing, August, 1997
10 9 8 7 6

 REGISTERED TRADEMARK—MARCA REGISTRADA

LIBRARY OF CONGRESS CATALOGING-IN-PUBLICATION DATA: is available

ISBN: 0-452-27801-5

Printed in the United States of America
Set in New Baskerville
Designed by Eve L. Kirch

A NOTE TO THE READER

This publication describes the author's opinion regarding the subject matter herein. It is sold with the understanding that the publisher and author are not engaged in rendering any professional service. If expert assistance is required, the services of a qualified professional should be obtained.

BOOKS ARE AVAILABLE AT QUANTITY DISCOUNTS WHEN USED TO PROMOTE PRODUCTS OR SERVICES. FOR INFORMATION PLEASE WRITE TO PREMIUM MARKETING DIVISION, PENGUIN PUTNAM INC., 375 HUDSON STREET, NEW YORK, NEW YORK 10014.

CONTENTS

ACKNOWLEDGMENTS

My mother and father worked long and hard so that succeeding generations of their family could have more freedom and more choices. They did it on faith and they achieved a profound goal. I am grateful to them not only for my life, but for the future of our family.

I am asked how an unknown, self-published book made it into the mainstream. It wasn't due to a chain of events, but to a chain of marvelous people. To all of them I offer my heartfelt thanks. Ian Thomson, Paul Cohen, Tom Peters, Irv Homer of WWDB radio in Philadelphia, and Nancy Austin all helped make the self-published edition a success. I am particularly indebted to Nancy for her spirited writing about my work, for contributing the kind of foreword authors only dream of, and for helping me keep my marbles while getting this book out.

My enterprising editor, Julia Serebrinsky, found me—not the other way around. I thank her for her patience and enthusiasm. She skillfully helped shape the book while respecting my message and my "voice." Special thanks go to Arnold Dolin, my publisher at Plume, for making a powerful commitment to a first-time author.

I wouldn't be doing what I love most if not for my online family at *The Motley Fool*: David and Tom Gardner, Erik Rydholm, Gabrielle

Loperfido, Jill Kianka, and a raft of other Fools. They adopted my *Ask the Headhunter* forum as the only noninvestment content on *The Motley Fool* in early 1995—but only after I proved it was Foolish. I have ridden on their coattails. They have generously given me complete editorial freedom and unequivocal trust in a medium where the Wise run scared and only true Fools dare risk it all. I've never worked with a smarter or more gracious bunch of people, online or off. I love them all.

There would be no book called *Ask the Headhunter* were it not for my agent, Suzanne Gluck. Her masterful negotiating skills, her wisdom, and her gentle nature make her an author's ideal partner. She and her able team at ICM, Marsinay Smith and Sloan Harris, have my gratitude. I can't imagine ever doing this again without them.

Special thanks go to Mel Parker, Bob Mecoy, Tom Colgin, and Denise Marcil for the warm welcome and the acknowledgment each of them so generously gave me.

To all my clients and the people I have placed with them, thanks for sharing your problems and challenges, and thanks for your trust and your business.

Several people are due thanks for their assistance with the book this one grew out of, *The New Interview Instruction Book.* My good friend Jeff Pierce shared his profound but totally unscientific observations about cows, and Jack Canty taught me the difference between being in charge and being in control. Eric Szantai, Richard Albanese, and Sam Spurlock provided much needed technical and moral support. Jeff Hirsch and his crew at Whitehall Printing in Naples, Florida, made that self-published book shine. No book succeeds without notice from the media, and a long list of publications helped in this regard, among them Tom Peters's *On Achieving Excellence,* Peter Drucker's *Leader to Leader, Electronic Engineering Times, Bottom Line Business, Working Woman,* and Merrill Lynch's *Business Insights* to name a few. Finally, to all the readers—individual job hunters and corporate employers—who bought and used *The New Interview Instruction Book,* thanks. Those of you who called, wrote or e-mailed to share your successes will never know how much your kind words continue to mean to me.

Special thanks are due Michael Freilich for listening like only a friend can, and for his always sage advice. Bob Golombik gets the attendance award for being there almost every day, prodding me with his wit, suggestions, observations, and baby stories—even though we've met only once.

My most important guides on this journey have been the readers of the online *Ask the Headhunter*. Their thousands of questions and postings have made the forum a rich source of understanding about what it's like to search for, identify, and profitably do a job in America today.

Some would argue that our willingness to take risks diminishes with age. But certain events force us to face change by creating more of it. The growth of my family did it for me. It prompted me to stop everything else I was doing and write this book. I thank my wife, Debby, for her enthusiasm, faith, and encouragement, and for her incredible patience while I "risked something that matters." As for Luke and Emma, well, when you're old enough to read this I hope you'll also just be learning that it's okay to take risks to do what's important to you (and I hope your father will be smart enough to know when to get out of the way and let you). Finally, I thank The Big Man Upstairs for always lending me grace.

READERS' NOTE

In an effort to avoid assaulting the reader with mixed gender pronouns, the masculine pronoun is used predominantly in this book. All the ideas apply equally to women and men.

FOREWORD

Nancy K. Austin

Years ago, an executive with a reputation as a superb judge of talent told me his "secret" to hiring the right people: He picked good drivers. About halfway through an interview, he would hand the keys of his Taurus to the astonished applicant and suggest a short spin around the block. He wanted, he said, to see how she would handle things behind the wheel. The executive figured that the way the candidate responded—first, to the invitation to go for a drive, then to whatever the trip might offer—was a reasonable proxy for how she would handle the stresses and surprises of business.

All twaddle, of course, but even hiring managers who would never dream of pulling such a stunt will confess to using a few offbeat strategies to smoke out the "real" person behind the tailored suit and word-perfect resume. They try to trick people by asking gimmicky questions: *How many Ping-Pong balls would it take to fill this room? If you knew you had only a year to live, what would you do differently? Can a man legally marry his widow's sister?* (Hint: If a man has a widow, he's too dead to marry anyone.)

Alas, these and a slew of other equally vexing pop quizzes serve only to throw already twitchy candidates for a loop *(What's your favorite color? With whom would you like to be stranded on a desert island?).* Even worse, putting applicants through such an ordeal tells the employer nothing— *nothing at all*—about a candidate's value to the organization. Oops, wasn't that supposed to be the point of the whole exercise?

Now we have a potent countermeasure in *Ask the Headhunter,* which liberates job hunters and employers alike from the folly and folklore of Ye Olde Interview Code. Its advice is radical, proven, and indispensable. As Nick Corcodilos (whose own headhunting credentials lend his book its insider feel) says, "interviewing is not about where you see yourself in five years. It is not about your weaknesses or your strengths. It is not about your most challenging experience or greatest accomplishment. *Interviewing is about the job.*"

Trouble is, this clarion idea is so shockingly simple that it can be difficult to understand. Think about it this way: Companies everywhere seek the kind of colleague—executive, marketing honcho, software engineer, caregiver—who can solve real problems and deliver profitable results. But most interviews are a big waste of time; that's why busy managers bring in headhunters who dump the tricks and the tea leaves and concentrate on assessing every ounce of capability and fit. They keep one thing uppermost in mind: Can this candidate do the job?

For applicants, then, solid homework is mandatory. No more breezing into an interview relying on charm, a new Brioni and a good line of patter. A serious candidate will take control and demonstrate an understanding of the company's operations, its standing in the marketplace, and its strategic and tactical problems. The right candidate offers real help and real solutions, the way a consultant makes professional recommendations to a client. "The winning candidate," Corcodilos tells us, "goes into the interview and does the job."

I wish I'd had this lifesaver of a book years ago, when I faced my first "big" interview as a newly minted MBA. In what turned out to be the accurately named "stress interview," half a dozen executives surrounded me, barking out questions and interrupting my attempts to answer. (It's a method favored by certain consulting firms, investment-banking houses and cops; intimidation, not enlightenment, is the goal here.) But there's a much better way. If you're job hunting, don't even think of setting up another interview until you read this book. And if you're looking to hire the best talent around, *Ask the Headhunter* will save you oceans of time, trouble, and aggravation. Then, when you and your candidate have found each other, it's time to ask the least gimmicky question of all: *When can you start?*

INTRODUCTION

When I started the *Ask the Headhunter* forum on America Online in April 1995 a smart, talented fellow wrote to tell me what seems to be, sadly, a common story. After a frustrating year of job hunting, he paid a firm several thousand dollars to mass mail his résumé to three thousand different companies in his field.

The outcome shocked him. "I haven't gotten even one reply, out of *three thousand* résumés and cover letters!" He was further distressed at having to come up with another five thousand dollars to hire a "job search" counselor to help with his quest for work. With nowhere else to turn—he had tried everything—he was putting himself in hock and grasping at straws.

This is the screeching halt the careers of millions of American workers have come to.

What's going on here? The media tells you that companies are downsizing and good jobs are disappearing. Experts on the United States economy, however, suggest otherwise. Robert J. Samuelson, writing in *Newsweek**, points out that since 1979 America created twenty-six million jobs and absorbed 95 percent of new workers. The unemployment rate, in fact, has not increased since 1979—it's

*Newsweek, July 29, 1996.

actually lower. The economy is getting stronger and American business is quite healthy. Companies are hiring. In fact, your chances of winning the right job are excellent, if you know how to position yourself as a profitable hire.

Yet since I wrote the original, self-published edition of this book a few years ago, I've heard stories of helplessness and frustration from thousands of job hunters. And they all share the same problem: while they're good at the work they do, they just can't navigate the murky employment system that seems bent on isolating them from the managers who need to hire them. No matter what industry they're in or where they live, the roadblock is always the same: "Send us your résumé and cop a chill. Don't call us, we'll call you. Next?"

Don't accept this deadly sentence issued by human resources departments across America. By applying a few simple concepts used by headhunters, you can not only beat the system but win the kind of job you once thought was unattainable.

The employment system, which has brainwashed you into accepting its methods, is run by people who have absolutely no vested interest in your goals, or in an employer's. That Byzantine machine that chews up and spits out job descriptions, want ads, résumés, job candidates, interview appointments and rejection letters is useless and defunct. When you mail out a hundred résumés and get no replies and every time a hiring manager finds a stack of five hundred résumés on his desk, the system fails. When a company trusts personnel clerks who know nothing about engineering to select the engineers the firm will hire something stinks. The right people aren't being hired and work is going begging while talented workers ride the employment system treadmill.

How does this system seduce an otherwise smart, productive professional like you into compliance? First, by being pervasive and intimidating. It confronts you daily through countless want ads, and it threatens you with the millions of your competitors it is soliciting. Second, it asserts itself at a point in your life when you're most vulnerable—when you need a new job. There's just too much at stake for you to buck the people who seem to be in control, so you politely answer idiotic questions like, "Where do you see yourself in five years?" when what you *really* want to say is, "Does this company *keep* people for five years?" But perhaps the main reason you accept the rules is because there seems to be no other choice.

Ask the Headhunter is your new alternative. This book will help you get what you want by helping you understand what an employer needs. For decades, headhunters have known that the traditional approach to hiring the right people is deeply flawed. We have created an approach to matching the right person with a job that is so effective, employers pay us to circumvent the counterproductive policies of their own human resources departments. We get the job done. We find the right person for a job quickly and with minimal fuss and bother. Unlike the bureaucratic processes of the secure, salaried human resources manager, our methods work because they have to. If they don't, we don't eat. It's as simple as that. And headhunters eat well. Good headhunters cut to the essentials—we deliver the job candidate who can prove he can do the work and do it profitably for himself and for the employer.

The immediate problem most job hunters face is that they can't hire a headhunter. Headhunters work only for companies, identifying and recruiting the new employees they need. That's why I wrote this book—to give you access to a resource most people can't get even if they could afford it.

Thousands of job hunters and employers have already learned how to beat the system through *Ask the Headhunter* workshops and the online *Ask the Headhunter* forum. You can use the headhunter's approach yourself to find and win the right job, without getting lost amidst the noise and nonsense of the frantic job market. Keep in mind that beating the system at its own game is a headhunter's full-time business, so learning these methods will take some dedicated effort on your part.

This book will teach you how the headhunter prepares and coaches a candidate to *do the job to win the job*, right in the interview. You'll learn how to clearly demonstrate that you can tackle the challenges an employer faces and add value to his bottom line. In other words, you'll avoid that "we'll-get-back-to-you" attitude that surfaces when a manager can't figure out whether hiring you would be a profitable investment.

There's no magic to this. To get a particular manager's attention, become an expert in his business, understand the work he needs done, and find out how he would want you to do it. Then walk in and prove to him that you're going to make his business more successful.

Sound like a lot of work? Well, so is that job you want. Why should convincing a manager to hire you be any less challenging than the job itself? It's up to *you* to prove your value to every employer you meet. Employers won't figure it out for themselves. Yet that's what your strictly historical résumé* is begging them to do, and the traditional interview can't help. They won't ask you to demonstrate your worth because they, too, have been brainwashed to conduct a mindnumbing interview rather than a roll-up-your-sleeves working meeting where the two of you can tackle a live problem that will reveal whether you're going to be a profitable employee. That's what I call *The New Interview.*

Why do you need to learn about *The New Interview?* Because companies are rethinking the relationship between people, work, and profitability. I originally wrote this book, which was called *The New Interview Instruction Book,* to help the job hunter, but employers have started adopting *The New Interview* concepts to help them reinvent their own approach to hiring. Among the hundreds of companies already using the book are Walt Disney World, Microsoft, Marriott, Blue Cross, MCI, Becton Dickinson, Mobil, and First Union Bank; and smaller businesses like Edison Brothers Stores, VECO Engineering and Rhino Records. Companies like these expect job candidates to step up to the plate and do the job in the interview. Are you ready to take that kind of control?

Machiavelli once suggested that the way to succeed in any endeavor is to rely only on those resources over which you have control, and not to count on those over which you don't. When you

---

*If you want to understand resumes in a radically new way, read my *Resume Blasphemy* article on the online Ask the Headhunter.

shoot one thousand résumés through the mail or across the internet, you have no control over who will read them or who will respond to you (if anyone). Could there even be one thousand jobs you would actually want? Do you know enough about them to decide? One thousand blind shots at success—blind because there's no way on earth you could prepare quickly enough for the one you might actually interview for. No control at all. Nothing to count on. That essentially random first step starts you down the road to your own interview funeral.

So what does a serious job hunter do? Take control the best way you know how—the way the headhunter does. Start your job search the same way you start your work day: with an assessment of exactly what work the employer needs done. Apply your considerable skills and talents to doing the necessary research and planning. In other words, figure out what it will take to do the job successfully. Then, when you meet the employer, don't wait for anyone to prod you: do the job, right there in the interview. Because if you don't, the candidate I coached will.

CHAPTER 1

The Headhunter's Radical Art of Interviewing

The Work-Interview Connection

Ask the Headhunter will teach you how to take control of the most important aspect of your job hunt—the interview. It will show you how to select and prepare for the interview that leads to the right job. The main idea is clear and simple: if you are good at doing your work, you can use the same skills to win your next job. This book will show you how. The concepts and methods discussed on the following pages are all based on practical experience I have gained during many years as a headhunter—experience you can use to help you find your next job. These concepts and methods may seem radical, but I assure you that they work.

Ask the Headhunter is intended for use by workers at all levels of responsibility, from executives to middle managers to individual contributors and support staff in just about any industry. If you are looking for a new job, this book can help you.

Here are some important things a headhunter knows that you should learn before your next job interview:

- Most interviews are a waste of time.

- Personnel departments don't hire people.

- Insiders have the best shot at the job.

- Answering interview questions is the least likely way to win a job offer.

- There aren't hundreds of jobs out there for you, so you shouldn't send out hundreds of résumés.

- Being good at your job is more important than being good at interviewing.

- People fail at interviews when they act like a job candidate rather than an employee.

- The employer wants to hire you.

- Interviews are about one thing: the work.

- Interviews should not be interrogations.

- Never enter an interview without the intent and means of controlling it.

- The employer wants you to solve his problems.

- You must *interview the employer* after you receive a job offer.

- The most important thing to do in an interview is *do the job.*

Your next interview should be an enjoyable, rewarding meeting with an employer who shares your excitement about the work you do. It should be an opportunity for you to demonstrate your skills and abilities, and an opportunity for the employer to get help in solving his problems. It should be the start of a new job where you can work profitably for yourself and for your employer. This book will show you how to turn what "should be" into reality.

The first three chapters show why the traditional methods of job hunting and interviewing don't work. Until you understand how America's employment system has brainwashed job hunters, you'll never be able to avoid common career-crippling mistakes. Subsequent chapters explore the concepts and methods that headhunters depend on to successfully place the right person in the right job. Employers willingly pay headhunters handsome fees for this knowledge and expertise. Finally, the book will teach you how *you* can use these proven headhunters' techniques to win job offers.

Your Own Private Headhunter

I wrote this book because I realized that just about anyone can benefit from an understanding of certain powerful job hunting and interviewing concepts that I have learned during many years as a headhunter.

A headhunter (or executive search firm) is an independent consultant who is hired by a company to find specialized workers. The headhunter himself is usually a specialist in his industry. The workers he finds and "places" may be executives, managers, or staff. The headhunter earns a fee equal to between 20 percent and 35 percent of the annual compensation of the person he places in a job.

As a successful headhunter, I have a unique education in how and why companies hire people. Long ago I learned that the way headhunters approach filling a job is very different from the way most people hunt for a job. The differences are glaring. Even the smartest job hunters will make the same mistakes over and over again. They learn slowly, because they practice job hunting only once every few years. After I started working as a headhunter, my education about job hunting was greatly accelerated. It had to be. If I didn't fill several jobs each month, I wasn't going to earn a living. I practiced my skills full-time, and I became quite good at my work within a year. After a few years, I was an expert.

Over the years I met many workers who were exceptional at what they did for a living. However, in spite of their professional skills, they were not very good at interviewing. Many of them failed to win job offers because *interviewing was not their job*. Since it was clearly *my* job, I developed a brief interviewing guide for the qualified candidates I sent to my clients that explained everything I had learned about what makes a company want to hire a job candidate.

That guide has grown into the book you now hold in your hands—a powerful tool that can help *you* win *your* next job.

The Brilliant Engineer Who Couldn't Get a Job

The first version of this guide was part of my desperate effort to help a job hunter who had the worst time of finding a job of anyone I'd ever encountered. Bob was a computer engineer whose exceptional skills were a rarity. He could quickly find and fix complex problems in enormous computer programs that were written by other people. Bob was very exact in his work, and he enjoyed doing it. Engineers like him were in great demand, and there were precious few of them around.

I met Bob early in my headhunting career while I was doing a search for a client. Although Bob was not the right person for the job, I liked him and I recognized how valuable his skills were, so I sent him out to meet several of my other clients. The outcome each time was negative. No one wanted to hire him. And Bob wasn't very surprised. He said he'd always had a problem getting job offers.

This made no sense to me, given Bob's outstanding skills. I started asking a lot of questions. I talked with Bob and with the clients who had turned him away. I couldn't believe my ears: this talented engineer, who was a very friendly guy to boot, had no idea about what he should say and do in an interview! Not even the most obvious things! Well, at least they were obvious to a headhunter.

For example, upon completing an interview for a job he really wanted, Bob never explicitly told the employer that he wanted the job.*

---

*Don't laugh at this. I am continually amazed at how rare is the interviewee who clearly and explicitly tells the interviewer, "I want this job." Too many job hunters convince themselves that it's improper to make this statement. A seasoned sales executive recently argued with me that he didn't "want the interviewer to think I'm desperate," even though he really wanted a particular job. He failed to do the most important thing in an interview: convince the employer in no uncertain terms that he wanted the job. He also failed to get an offer.

Bob hated going on interviews. He forced himself, but his anxiety overshadowed his technical skills when he met with a prospective employer. Here was a talented, highly paid engineer who loved his work but couldn't interview to save his life.

"Bob, what happens?" I asked him one afternoon.

"Well, I always answer all of the interviewer's questions," he said.

"What else?" I prodded.

"That's about it. I'm polite, and I tell the interviewer everything he wants to know."

"Do you tell him you want the job, after the interview is over?" I suggested.

"Well, that's up to him. I can't tell him to hire me. If he doesn't want to hire me, I really wouldn't want to work there."

"But, Bob," I responded with amazement, "if you can't make that commitment to the employer, *why on earth would he want to hire you?*"

That did it. If Bob was missing this one basic point, what else was he missing? I sat down and wrote out four pages of principles Bob should think about before going into an interview, and four pages of things he should say and do during the interview. He read it that evening and called me at home, bubbling with excitement.

"Why didn't you tell me this before?" he demanded. "I've always hated interviews because I'm asked so many questions that have nothing to do with my work. It's a game, and I hate that. I feel like I'm being interrogated and I never know what to say. I've always wished an interviewer would just let me show him what I can do rather than ask about stuff I'm just not good at talking about.

"In my fifteen years as an engineer no one ever taught me any of the things in your guide. You make interviewing sound like it's no more complicated than doing your job. And I know that I'm good at my job."

Two days later, I sent Bob off to what must have been his fourth or fifth interview in as many weeks. The client called me immediately after their meeting to offer Bob a management job at a considerable increase in salary. He complimented me on sending him a qualified worker who was clearly ready and motivated to do the job.

That little guide helped many candidates win job offers. And it helped me earn handsome fees from droves of satisfied clients.

Do Headhunters Have a Secret?

I wrote that original guide because, as a headhunter, I needed a simple, powerful and efficient way to teach job candidates how to prepare for their interviews. I expanded the guide into a book because I recognized that many people can benefit from a detailed understanding of the concepts good headhunters use to place good workers.

I hear the same frustrating job hunting story all the time: "I've sent out dozens of résumés and I've interviewed with lots of companies, but I can't get an offer!"

Most people are mystified about how to turn an interview into a job offer, but they needn't be. Headhunters have figured out these "secrets" and use them successfully every day.

What most job hunters don't recognize is that in today's competitive business world *traditional interviews are a waste of time.* And what goes on behind the scenes in the hiring process draws people deeper and deeper into a dysfunctional administrative maze that keeps them focused on all the wrong things.

When people ask me "What's the headhunter's secret?" I tell them, "Stop trying to get a job like everyone else. Stop reading want ads, stop sending out résumés, stop going on interviews, and stop waiting by the phone. That's the headhunter's secret."

I usually get a blank stare in response, followed by something like "Don't tell me what *not* to do. Tell me what *to do.*"

"Believe me," I always reply, "what *not* to do is just as important as what you must do. Now, as for what you must do: interview only for the few jobs that are absolutely right for you, talk directly to the employer himself, meet with him and *do the job,* and you will be hired."

Well, this mystifies people even more. "How do I do all that? And besides, how do I *do the job* before I get the job?"

It all comes down to learning how to fish.

Learning to Fish

There are many books about job hunting, and they offer advice about writing résumés, preparing for interviews, doing interviews, and negotiating compensation. Most of these books are recipe books. They provide you with lists of all the things you should do to get a job. Most books on interviews will give you a list of the common interview questions and explain how you should answer them. They also give you lists of all the things you should definitely talk about, and the things you should avoid discussing.

One of the problems with this approach is that the job hunter can easily become overwhelmed. Such books try to cover every possible situation. There is often so much advice that the candidate runs the risk of appearing stiff or unnatural during the interview, because he's trying to remember and do "all the right interview things." In the worst case, the candidate becomes confused and inarticulate. Some people become so overwhelmed that they just freeze up.

These advice books can be useful if they are approached in the way I've described them: as recipe books. You wouldn't prepare every dish listed in a cookbook for a single meal, and you shouldn't want to use every "technique" listed in a job hunting book during a single interview. It would be overwhelming.

How do you know which techniques to use in your interviews and which to discard?

You must let your philosophy about your work be your guide. This book will help you to develop that philosophy. I am going to not only teach you interviewing techniques but also show you how to *think* about interviewing and about your work. This will enable you to *use the tools that are best for you* when you interview.

It has been said that if you give a man a fish, you feed him for one day. If you teach him how to fish, you feed him for the rest of his life. This book will do more than help you win your next job. It will teach you how to present yourself as the kind of worker an employer will always want to hire.

Ask the Headhunter is designed to help you understand interviewing in a new way. It will teach you to approach interviewing in the same way you approach doing your job, because there is almost no difference between the two. If you are good at doing your work, you can be good at interviewing.

> This book contains a handful of very powerful ideas. They are so important that I will repeat them many times in different contexts. I will show you how to apply these ideas to almost every aspect of job hunting, although the focus will be on interviewing.

The Employment Industry Follies

Hunting for your next job is a very personal and a very practical task. It has little to do with interviews, résumés, networking, thank-you notes, personnel departments, or headhunters. Don't let anyone confuse you. Hunting for your next job is about one thing: *doing the job.* That means understanding the job, doing it, doing it the way the employer wants it done, and doing it profitably for you and for your employer. Anyone who tells you there is some trick to finding your next job is wrong. Employers today are tired of people who want a job they can't do or don't care about. There's too much focus on *getting a job* and not enough on *doing the work.*

One of the aims of this book is to help undo most of what the *employment industry* has taught you. Make no mistake—the employment process in the United States has become an industry of its own. To undo what it has taught you, we will have to change your attitude about companies and jobs, and about how you view yourself and your work.

> The first thing you must do is to approach interviewing from your standpoint—the standpoint of a person trying to land a job—not that of the people between you and the person who's going to hire you.

You will encounter many people who are not really the person who will hire you—they are the go-betweens who want you to hunt for a job in a way that's convenient for *them*. These employment industry people include career counselors, human resources experts, personnel representatives, job description writers, want ad composers, résumé preparers, interviewers, and personnel agencies. I call all these people *personnel jockeys*.

No personnel jockey will ever be as concerned about you or about the job as the hiring manager. You'll encounter some good ones, but understand that most personnel jockeys are zombies. They go about their work mindlessly focusing on abstractions because they don't understand the work you do. So they push paper instead. Stay away from them, because their way of doing things centers on getting you to play their game.

Their game is all the garbage they keep in their file drawers, like want ads, résumés, forms, applications, job descriptions, questionnaires, rejection letters, contracts, federal guidelines, and legal mumbo jumbo. What personnel jockeys want is for you to help them push paper around, because that's their job. To do their job, they have to convince you to act like every other job candidate, so that they can turn you into another piece of paper. That makes it easy for them to cram you into a file drawer. If you act like every other job candidate *they will file you* and *you will never find your next job.*

If you think I'm being too harsh on personnel jockeys, consider the fact that companies devote huge budgets to human resources departments, but they still turn to headhunters to fill job openings. I have placed candidates in jobs—and earned fees—when the human resources manager already had—but ignored—the candidate's résumé. Nowadays, human resources departments and internal recruiting functions are among the first to get chopped when a downsizing occurs. They're just not doing the job.

As a headhunter, I learned to approach the job hunt very exactly and very ferociously, avoiding most personnel jockeys at all costs.* I did all my work in advance, before I scheduled an interview. Since I usually worked on contingency, I only made a living if I *filled* the job and, due to the guarantees I gave my clients, I got to keep my money only if the candidate *was right for the job.* So I worked very carefully. I was exact. And, because I was competing not only with other job applicants but also with other headhunters, I had to be ferocious and fearless.

That meant going straight to the hiring authority, the person who was spending money from his budget to hire someone. It meant understanding *the job behind the description* and exactly what the manager needed to make his department more profitable. It meant finding out what the politics were. Working fast. Making sure I understood the job before I did anything else. Making sure I had the right candidate. Making sure the candidate was *completely prepared* for the interview. Making sure the candidate was *the solution to the manager's problem.*

These are the headhunter's methods, and you can benefit by using them. Be exact. Don't send out two hundred résumés and apply for two hundred jobs. There are not two hundred jobs out there for you. Don't waste your time. Do what a headhunter does, and do it like your next paycheck depends on it, because it does. Find the few right jobs and go after those exactly and fearlessly.

Be ferocious. Don't be afraid of, or waste your time with, people whose job is to screen hundreds of candidates. Push them out of the way. Let them work on the *other* candidates for the job. Blow every

---

*As with everything in life, there are no absolutes. There are some very good personnel workers out there who do much more than just practice the inane, inadequate procedures of the employment industry. But, I must tell you that among the hundreds of "personnel workers" I have met or talked with, I can count on one hand the ones I truly respect. My advice is to not take chances with personnel jockeys; the odds are against you.

other candidate out of the water. Go after the job as if you already have it. Get in front of the manager you would be reporting to and show him you can do the job and do it profitably.

That's what this book is about. Most other books on this topic are written by personnel jockeys. Human resources experts. Corporate stuffed shirts who spend their lives managing other people who spend their time pushing paper and filling out forms. They don't hire anyone. They would have you think they do, but all they do is process the candidates that managers decide to hire.

Those self-proclaimed experts will teach you how to play their game.

I am going to teach you what you need to do to *win the job offer* so that you can decide whether to *hire yourself a new employer.*

Why Do You Need This Book?

You need this book because almost everything you have been taught about interviewing for a job is wrong. If what you had been taught was right, you would not be worried about the outcome of your next interview. If you're concerned about what's going to happen the next time you meet with a manager to talk about a job, you need this book. *Ask the Headhunter:*

- Teaches you how to become a powerful candidate by building an attitude about your *work* that will help you win job offers.
- Teaches you how to use the *Four Questions* to distinguish a right interview from a wrong one.
- Explains how *trying to get a job* can land you in the wrong job.
- Shows you where and how to gain the *inside edge* you need to interview confidently and convincingly.
- Shows you how to *control* your next interview to your advantage.
- Reveals the difference between *doing the interview* and *doing the job,* and explains what to do to win offers.

- Shows you how to capitalize on the only thing you and the interviewer have in common: *the job*.
- Makes an employer see you as a valued employee before the interview is over by making you the *solution to his problems*.
- Gets you on the manager's short list of candidates by showing you how to give *compelling proof* that you can do the job.
- Puts you in a powerful position to optimize any job offer.

Let *Ask the Headhunter* guide you through your interviews.

The Six Secrets of the New Interview

There is nothing special, or even very useful, about the traditional interview. However, in what I call the New Interview, there are Six Secrets you should be aware of. Every good headhunter understands these basic tenets of his work and uses them every day—you should, too.

1. Insiders have the best shot at the job.
2. The real matchmaking is done before the interview.
3. The interview is an invitation to do the job.
4. The employer wants to hire you, and he will help you win the interview.
5. The boss wants one thing from you: he wants you to solve a problem *profitably*.
6. You will win the job by doing it—that is, by solving the problem in the interview.

Let's look closely at what the Six Secrets of the New Interview really mean.

1. Insiders have the best shot at the job.

Other things being equal, the boss will hire someone he knows before he hires someone he does not know. Why? Because he has more information about people he already knows, like other company employees, than he has about you, and the information he has is more reliable.

Part of a headhunter's job is to build his candidate's reputation within a company before the candidate goes on the interview. You can accomplish this for yourself. In the sections that follow, we will discuss how you can make an employer perceive you as a valued employee rather than an outsider.

2. *The real matchmaking is done before the interview.*

The challenge of matching a worker with a job is addressed *before* the interview, not during the interview. Just as a lawyer never asks a witness a question in court unless the lawyer already knows the answer, a headhunter never sends a candidate to an interview unless the headhunter already knows the candidate can do the job. You must ensure the same fit for yourself. You cannot match yourself to a job unless you know *exactly* what the parameters of the job are before you walk into the interview.

3. *The interview is an invitation to do the job.*

Most people treat an interview like an interrogation. One person asks questions, the other gives answers. This is wrong. Headhunters go out of their way to structure interviews to avoid this very unfavorable scenario.

An interview is a meeting between you and the employer—you are equals. The traditional notion of the all-powerful interviewer and the deferential candidate is hogwash. Unfortunately, this notion is promoted each time someone says that a candidate *was interviewed by* an employer.

The root of the word *interview* means *between*; it does not imply that one person is doing something to another, or that the employer has power over you, the candidate. An interview is an exchange of information between two or more people. The only power either of you has is the power you have each *granted* to the other. If you grant an employer the power to intimidate you and interrogate you under a hot light, then that's your decision. Just realize that you're exacerbating your fear and anxiety—and the employer can smell it. Employers don't hire fearful candidates.

There is one power you and the employer share. If you can capitalize on it, you will turn the interview into a decisive problem-solving experience that will make the employer view you and treat you like a member of his team. This power lies in your choice to work together with the employer to get the job done. This means avoiding interrogations. It means *doing the job* in the interview. We will talk more about how you can put this power to work and thereby avoid *getting interviewed* in the traditional sense.

4. The employer wants to hire you, and he will help you win the interview.

This is precisely why the employer is meeting with you. Every headhunter knows that. Once you understand this fundamental fact, you will realize that you really have been brainwashed. The headhunter counts on the employer being ready to hire the candidate. *So should you.* If the employer hires you, he wins, too. He can stop interviewing, and he can start earning the profits that having you on the job will yield.

Give the employer what a good headhunter gives him: proof that you can do the work. He wants you to be the right candidate. Half your battle is won. More than any other single fact about interviewing, this should make you feel relaxed, comfortable, and powerful in an interview when you are looking for a new job.

5. The boss wants one thing from you: he wants you to solve a problem profitably.

Every employer who interviews you has a problem: a job that needs doing. Most candidates don't solve the boss's problem because they don't know what the problem is, and because they're too busy "doing the interview." That's what keeps headhunters in business—job candidates who can't identify and solve the boss's problem.

A headhunter makes sure his candidate knows *exactly what problem he has to solve to win an offer.* He also knows how any suggested solution will make the employer more successful and profitable. If one of your predecessors had proved they could solve the employer's problem this way, the employer would not be talking to you.

Solve one or more of the manager's problems during the interview. See what happens.

6. You will win the job by doing it—that is, by solving the problem in the interview.

You will not win the job by talking about it. Managers end interviews with "we'll get back to you" when they can't decide whether to hire you. That's because they're not sure you can do the job. What more compelling way is there to convince a manager to hire you than to do the job the way he wants it done right there in front of him? If you waste your meeting answering questions rather than doing the job, you will lose that job to another candidate who was well prepared to *do the job.*

Good headhunters know these secrets and apply them all the time. They treat all interviews as practical, problem-solving meetings with a purpose, and *the purpose is to show that a job candidate can do a job* so that he will be hired. The headhunter devotes all of his energy to achieving this purpose.

I have shared these ideas over the years with job candidates I've sent to meet my clients. It is crucial for candidates to recognize how important they are to the employer. I want my candidates to see interviews for what they are: opportunities for skilled people to demonstrate to an employer the best way a job can be done.

These ideas will change your job hunt in some very important ways if you put them to work. Freed from the banality of the traditional interview, you will form a relaxed attitude about interviewing and develop the confidence and power that a talented worker should have. You will blossom from a job candidate into the solution to a manager's problem.

What an Employer Really Wants from You

After sitting through one confusing interview after another, it's easy to become confused about what an employer really wants. Does he want someone with the right personality, or someone who has a certain kind of degree? Maybe the employer is looking for one "magic word" on your résumé. Or, maybe he's looking for the right body language.

The Vice President in Charge of Outcomes

By successfully interviewing and hiring the right people, Buck Adams, Vice President for a multinational telecommunications firm, has helped establish more than forty new companies in emerging markets around the world in just over two years. "Behavior, skills, personality—none of it by itself accurately predicts how well someone will do a job," Adams says. "None of it means you can perform. I reference the interview to the outcomes I need—to the work that must be done. I don't hire people because of what they say. I hire them because they can prove they can *do the work*!"

Ask Adams what his primary concern is when he interviews someone, and "Outcomes!" he says, without blinking an eye. No wonder.

A highly decorated retired air force officer, Adams served as commanding general of North American Air Defense Command (NORAD). You've probably heard of it—that mysterious, self-contained five-acre, seven-story facility deep in the heart of a granite mountain near Colorado Springs that supports the world's most sophisticated terrestrial and space-based attack-warning and communications system. His mission? To control outcomes.

Adams also flew 127 air combat missions in Vietnam, all of them successful. And he holds the world speed record in the SR-71 "Blackbird" spy plane flying between London and Los Angeles (three hours, forty-seven minutes). Today Buck Adams spends his time flying around the world overseeing company operations and searching for executives to run new telecommunications companies. One of his greatest challenges is to help *them* hire the right people. And guess what matters most to him?

Outcomes.

Can You Do the Work?

What an employer really wants—whether he realizes it consciously or not—is to know that you can produce the outcomes he needs. In other words, can you successfully do the work?

Maybe you have a nice personality. Maybe you have clever answers to interview questions. Maybe you were successful at your last job. But, can you do *this* work *now*?

The problem is, if the employer doesn't know how to get you to answer this question in the interview—and many employers don't—he won't hire you. He'll be left with an empty feeling, and you'll be left without a job offer.

Not long after I got into the headhunting business in 1979 in Silicon Valley, California, I learned why my clients paid me large fees to fill important positions. They weren't interested in fancy résumés or in people who could interview well. They paid me for just one thing: to bring them the one person who could do the job. They were concerned about *outcomes.*

This realization forever changed my point of view about job hunting. It's not about credentials. It's not about résumés. It's not about interviews. It's not about references or aptitude tests or your personality or whether someone likes you. Job hunting is about *the work.* Understanding it. Doing it. Doing it the way the employer needs to have it done. And doing it profitably.

Putting the Work in the Interview

Although interviewing is a very important management responsibility, it is a relatively infrequent task. Many managers hate interviewing because it takes them away from their primary work: it can be tiresome and time-consuming, and many managers aren't very good at it. In fact, like job hunters, they've been brainwashed. The questions and answers become repetitive. Candidates all start to look and sound alike. In the meantime, there's a job waiting to be done.

Most job candidates hate interviews because they can do their job better than they can do interviews. Even the most talented worker can suddenly find himself fumbling through an uncomfortable, misguided discussion that seems far removed from his expertise: doing his job.

"The traditional interview has been shown to have little or no statistical utility as a selection technique," says Annette Flippen, an organizational psychologist at Columbia University. "If more people would focus on proving they can do the work, the interview would better fulfill its purpose of matching people with the jobs that are right for them." An expert in how organizations make decisions, Flippen is convinced—as are many others in her field— that something critical is missing in the hiring ritual.

Hidden in this ancient, complex social interaction called interviewing is the one thing the employer and the candidate are really concerned about: the work. The candidate wants to *do it* and the employer wants to *get it done.* You may not be interviewing for a job at NORAD, where the safety of the world depends on the outcome of your work. You may not be the next executive Buck Adams hires to run a new telecommunications company. But you'd better learn how to peel away the parts of an interview that matter the least to a guy like Adams, so that you can focus on what matters most: your ability to do the work.

CHAPTER 2

Putting the Work in the Interview

What an Interview Is Really About

Employers and job candidates alike tend to get lost in the formalities of the interview. These formalities include a slew of standard interview questions that are almost meaningless, except that they produce a lot of anxiety. People forget that there are just a few core questions that an interview is intended to answer. All the other nerve-racking questions are mostly fluff. They can cost you the job if you let them become more important than they really are. In this chapter, I will discuss in detail what interviewing is really all about. I will teach you how to focus your interviews on what's important, and how to use your newfound understanding to make your interviews comfortable and successful.

Knowing *how to think* about job hunting is more important than just having a collection of techniques that you can whip out when you need them. You must consider your approach carefully before you act. You won't be doing this alone. We will walk together through some fundamental concepts that will help you to understand why the most common job hunting methods don't work. We'll also take a look at the misconceptions that may have caused you to waste your time in the past.

I don't expect you to change your way of thinking about finding a job just because I say you should. I am also not claiming that you will improve the way you interview if you just follow ten easy steps. But if you devote the energy required to think about and practice the ideas presented in this book, a big light should go on in your head, and job hunting will never be the same for you.

Most people don't know certain things about job hunting and interviewing because they don't do it for a living like a headhunter does. (If you've been out of a job for a long time, you might think hunting for a job is a full-time job. It's not. Don't let it become one.) The first thing the headhunter knows that you don't is this: interviewing is not about what you think it is about. Interviewing is not about being asked questions about yourself. It is not about your credentials or your past jobs. It is not about salaries. It is not about job descriptions. It is not about titles.

Interviewing is not about where you see yourself in five years. It is not about your weaknesses or your strengths. It is not about your most challenging experience or greatest accomplishments. It is not about wearing the right clothes or about being aggressive. It is not about answering questions or getting an offer.

Interviewing is about the job.

The Four Questions

You can judge every job opportunity by applying the Four Questions. The Four Questions will reveal your *knowledge, attitude,* and *ability* regarding a specific job. These are the true sources of success in any interview, because they are the things an employer needs to know.

1. Do you understand the job that needs to be done?
2. Can you do the job?
3. Can you do the job the way the employer wants it done?
4. Can you do the job profitably for the company?

If you can answer yes to each question and do so honestly, your chances of winning the job offer will be excellent.* Yet, one of the most frequent responses I hear from job hunters is, "Are you kidding? Answering those questions about every job I apply for would be a lot of hard work!" My reply is always the same: "So is any good job, isn't it? Why should anyone offer you the job if you won't do the hard work necessary to prove you're right for it?"

If you can answer yes to the Four Questions for a particular job, you will eliminate almost all doubt and anxiety from your mind when you enter the interview. You will be powerful, you will be relaxed, and you will be one of the best candidates the employer will meet *because you will know there is a match between you and the job.*

The Power of the Four Questions

The Four Questions will serve as your guide to many aspects of work, including finding work, winning the right job, doing your job, becoming better at your job, and keeping your job.

The Four Questions will help you *find* the right job by helping you to avoid the wrong jobs—as well as potentially disastrous interviews. Always keep in mind that if you are considering a work opportunity but cannot answer the Four Questions, you probably have not done your homework. My suggestion is, don't go on the interview at all—you'll bomb. If you've asked and answered the Four Questions and all the answers aren't yes, the job is not right for you or you're not right for the job. Because the Four Questions will give you an in-depth understanding of every job opportunity you consider, you'll be able to select only the jobs that are right for you. In turn, that understanding will give you an incredible edge over every other candidate.

---

*You may have noticed that a very important question seems to be missing: Is this a job you want to do? It's missing for a very good reason: you should already know whether you want the job before you go on the interview. We'll address this issue later.

How will the Four Questions help you *win* the right job? Because in the course of answering them all with a yes, you will:

- Mold your *knowledge* about the job and the employer's business into a compelling tool that will help you win an offer.
- Form an impressive *attitude* which, because it is soundly based on your knowledge about the job, will tell the employer that you're there to help solve his problems and to make his business more profitable if he hires you.
- Be prepared to demonstrate the relevant talents, skills, and *abilities* that will make you the most powerful candidate the employer meets.

Finally, the Four Questions will help you *do* your job, become better at it, and keep it by helping you to better understand how to:

- Fulfill the requirements of your job.
- Hone your skills and determine what if any new skills you'll need to acquire.
- Pinpoint what makes your work valuable to your employer.
- Measure how your work affects profitability.
- Present yourself as a talented worker who is promotable.
- Build and develop your confidence.
- Pave the road for your growth.

Check Your Attitude

This book offers a new approach to thinking about your work. What does that have to do with interviewing? Everything—because the attitude you reveal about your work in an interview tells an employer how you will likely tackle the job he wants to hire you to do.

Employers want workers who can focus on doing their work. After all, we spend much more time doing our work than doing interviews. But then, so do managers who interview prospective employees. Interviewing is really a very small part of our work lives. To get an employer's attention, focus on your job and your work, not on the interview.

Learn to see yourself not as a job seeker, but as a good worker: this is the way an employer wants to see you. If "I'm here to get a job" is the attitude you project in the interview, you will lose. Employers aren't in the business of giving out jobs. They're in business to produce a profitable product or service. And during an interview you want to act as if you're a person who's there to deliver profitable work. That attitude will make an employer hire you.

Because employers are not consciously aware of this at every point, your attitude is critical in leading them to a positive conclusion. A powerful work attitude will help you to talk with an employer about doing and winning a job; it will also help you to be an effective worker the employer will want to keep. And perhaps most important, this attitude reveals that you accept responsibility for proving your worth.

Take Responsibility

In many areas of our lives, we give up responsibility for things that are important to us, either out of habit or because someone offers us an easy way out. We like quick solutions. We want someone to tell us what the rules are so that we can follow them.

Many job hunters blindly follow someone else's rules as they conduct their job search. They believe that if they follow all the rules set up by personnel jockeys—reading ads, sending out résumés, sitting through interviews, and answering questions— they will be on the way to their next job. This kind of job hunter is deceiving himself. By relinquishing to an interviewer the responsibility for deciding whether a job is right for him the job hunter diminishes his own power.

Here's how a responsible job hunter would view an interview: I will not let someone interrogate me so that he can decide whether I can do a certain job. *I will decide whether I can do that job before I meet with the interviewer.* I will attend the interview so that I can show him what I can do and he can see why he needs to hire me. That's how I will demonstrate my respect for him and his business.

> I take full responsibility for being able to do the job before going on an interview. I don't need or want an interviewer to figure that out for me. And I have too much respect for him and for myself to make him figure it out for me.

Job hunters respond to want ads because it's easier than identifying good companies and calling on managers who might need help. Job candidates sit and answer questions because they don't know enough about the job to stand up in an interview and demonstrate that they can do it. The consequence of this attitude—"*you* figure out if this job is for me"—is that job hunters leave responsibility for their careers up to employers.

Good employers don't want this responsibility.

> By being *responsible* for your interviews and for the jobs you pursue, you will attain *control* over them.

Be the Right Candidate

The suggestions you will encounter in this book will not only help you to be the right candidate for a particular job, but also help you to be a good worker.

> The path from being "the right candidate" to "a good worker" lies in your understanding of the difference between someone who is out to *get a job* and a worker who is out to *do a job.* This is the single most important distinction between a rejected job hunter and a successful one.

If you want to meet the manager on his terms and at his level, and have a *meeting of the minds* with the employer rather than get interviewed by him, it is vital that you focus on the work you do. You can't do this if you're busy trying to beat the interview and get the job. You can only do it if you convince the manager that your goal is to do the work.

In selecting an employment opportunity, keep in mind that not all jobs will be "winnable" for you. Don't delude yourself. You have to be realistic. Ask anyone who has gone on five or ten interviews. How many offers did he get? If most interviews weren't a waste of time, the job hunter would have five or ten job offers to show for his trouble.

Most interviews are a waste of time because they are the wrong interviews. People typically go on interviews simply because they are invited. It takes a lot of research and a lot of thought to identify the *right* interviews to go on. If you go on the wrong interview for the wrong job, nothing will help you except luck. When someone tells me they went on an interview but did not win an offer, I always ask the same two questions: "Was it the right job? How do you know?"

Beware of claims that special interview techniques are the key to job offers. Some "employment experts" would have you believe that your interviewing skills are as important as your work abilities, and that with the right interview skills you can handle any interview. Their claims miss the point: companies seek people who can do the job, not people who are expert at doing interviews for any job that comes along. I urge you not to try to get as many interviews as you can; in fact, I suggest that you do the opposite: go on fewer interviews.

Don't be a clever candidate. Be the right candidate.

Don't Play Games: Do the Work and Win the Job

If you've already studied up on interviewing techniques, you're probably focusing too much on the interview process and too little on the work you want to be hired to do. Interview skills are not work skills. People often are hired just because they are clever interviewees. All that proves is that some employers are as haphazard about whom they will hire as job seekers are about whom they will interview with. Good luck to you and to the guy who hired you if you get your job this way. You'll both need it. More and more, managers tell me that there is little correlation between how well a candidate interviews and how well he does on the job. Lots of sharp interviewees turn out to be poor workers. Eventually, they end up paying the price by starting their job hunt again.

There's nothing wrong with preparing to meet someone and preparing to answer questions. But you will sell yourself short if your preparation is focused more than 10 percent on the formalities of interviewing. Ninety percent of your preparation should be spent on answering the Four Questions; that is, on understanding the employer's business, your skills, and your ability to do the work.

Does this mean that you must do more than read this book if you want to succeed at your next interview? That's exactly what it means. If you spend a few hours reading and studying the ideas in this book, you should spend several days studying the job for which you are applying. This book cannot teach you how to interview for the specific kind of work you do. Ideally, there would be a special interviewing book for every occupation; but there is not. You have to do that research for yourself.

Interviews are not stage shows; you won't be expected to do tricks. Consequently, you won't find me recommending a collection of fancy techniques designed to impress an interviewer who is more interested in style than substance. This is not to say that some interviewers won't expect a contrived performance from you. But in such interviews, it is up to you to turn a sideshow into a professional problem-solving meeting. Clever tricks won't accomplish that. Solid, commonsense business skills will enable you to put a bad interview on the right track. The same skills will help you to terminate an interview that is going nowhere fast.

Nothing is more frustrating to a good manager than a candidate who sits and spouts rehearsed answers to his questions; therefore, I will not offer you the "right" answers to "typical" interview questions. No interview is typical, unless you let it become so—and then you lose. Contrary to what authors suggest in books that list hundreds of clever answers to "typical" interview questions, an interview should never be a rote rehash of every other interview—otherwise, why not just hand the interviewer a copy of those pages? It isn't a game. You want to stand out, remember?

I can't help you if you believe in taking a shotgun approach to finding your next job. But, I *can* help you to improve your chances of winning the right offer for the right job by teaching you how to focus on *the work*. This attitude will make you the most powerful job candidate the employer ever meets.

The *Only* Way to Win a Job

If I haven't convinced you that everything you know about job hunting is wrong, and that the way the headhunter does it is right, perhaps I should tell you a bit more about the business of the headhunter. This will help you to see why the headhunter's approach is the *only* approach to finding and winning the right job.

I am often asked why headhunters are more successful at matching people and jobs than "regular" people. After all, who could be more motivated to land a good job than the person who's looking for one? The answer is obvious, and it illuminates the mistakes people make when they look for a job.

The headhunter is in business to make money. Unlike the job hunter, who might go through the job hunting process once every few years, the headhunter has to obtain many job offers, and he has to do it all the time. If there's a match between a worker and a job out there, he's going to find it. The headhunter is focused on one thing only: making a good placement. Because he is not distracted by the things that confuse the job hunter, the headhunter is able to concentrate on three goals:

1. Placing the right person in the right job.
2. Ensuring the new hire does the job well.
3. Building a reputation for making the right placements.

Headhunters use this approach because it pays off handsomely. They control the interview by defining the agenda so that it focuses employer and candidate on the work. They introduce employers only to candidates who are right for the job. They position the candidate as the solution to the employer's problems, and they leverage the approach to control negotiations at offer time. That's how head-hunters do it, and that's how you can do it.

The headhunter does not get stuck following someone's "rules of interviewing" or "rules of negotiating compensation." The tools a headhunter uses are flexible. The headhunter ignores what everyone else is doing and focuses instead on figuring out *what the job is, who controls it, and who can do the job profitably.*

Most job hunters read want ads, mail résumés, go blindly on interviews, and then wait by the phone. They're busy fooling around with a process that is designed to keep them away from the hiring manager, not to bring them together quickly. That's why a headhunter gets paid a lot of money to fill a job: because job hunters can't always find their own way to the waiting job. Using the headhunter's approach, you can find the best job for yourself on your own.

The concepts that we will discuss are deceptively simple when you first look at them. But in order to make them work, you have to make a great shift in your thinking. You have to forget about the interview for a while and focus on the work you do and the job you are seeking. That's what the headhunter does, because that is what's really important to the employer.

This approach will yield multiple benefits for you. First, the headhunter's approach will relax you and put you in control because while you may not be good at doing interviews, you are good at doing your job. Focusing on your work will help you in the interview. Second, it will enable you to narrow your job search. You will stop wasting time on jobs that are not right for you, because the Four Questions will help you quickly eliminate them. As a result, you will have fewer demoralizing interview experiences. Your sense of power and confidence over your job search will grow because you will be putting more energy and attention toward the few right jobs. Third, the headhunter's approach will turn you into the most valuable worker that a prospective boss can have—before he hires you. Finally, it will give you great leverage when it comes time to negotiate your job offer.

WORKSHEET 1:
ASSESS YOUR INTERVIEWS

Try to recall your last interview, and answer the following questions.

1. **How much of an insider are you at the company with which you just interviewed?**

   Add or subtract points as indicated depending on whether you agree (Yes) or disagree (No).

   _____ Prior to the interview, I knew at least one company employee [Yes +1 / No −1]

   _____ I know a person who is a vendor to or a customer of the company [Yes +1 / No −1]

   _____ I talked with at least two of these people about the job [Yes +3 / No −1]

   _____ At least one of these people spoke to the company about me [Yes +6 / No −1]

   For the next four parts, score the indicated number of points for each item you agree with.

2. **Did you have a meeting, or did you get interrogated?**

   _____ We talked about how my skills could solve the manager's problems [+2]

   _____ I felt powerful during the interview [+2]

   _____ The interviewer made me rather nervous [−1]

   _____ I know I answered several questions incorrectly[−1]

   _____ We discussed how this job affects the company's profits [+2]

   _____ I think I asked too many questions [−2]

_____ We spent a lot of the time talking about things other than the job [−2]

_____ The manager asked me to demonstrate how I do my work [+3]

3. **Do you think the employer really wants to hire you?**

_____ There's never any telling who an interviewer is going to hire [−2]

_____ I feel uncomfortable the minute I walk into any interview [−1]

_____ I think the manager really wants to hire someone else [−2]

_____ This is a very important job [+2]

4. **Are you a worker the employer needs to hire?**

_____ I don't understand why I haven't heard back yet [−3]

_____ The job wasn't really what I expected [−3]

_____ The manager and I worked together to solve a problem he was facing [+3]

_____ I didn't feel comfortable enough to actually tell the manager I wanted the job [−4]

5. **Did you get a real taste for the job?**

_____ I met at least two other people in the department [+3]

_____ I saw or actually used the tools I would use on the job [+3]

_____ We spent the entire interview in one room by ourselves [−3]

_____ I spent more time with Personnel than with the actual employer [−6]

Scoring: Add up your points. **28–31:** *You usually win an offer.* **23–27:** *You need to build more confidence or do more homework.* **19–22:** *You're not controlling your interviews.* **15–18:** *You're going on the wrong interviews.* **<15:** *You're waiting for someone to hand you a job.*

CHAPTER 3

Interview Follies: Why America's Employment System Doesn't Work

There Must Be a Better Way

Once upon a time, the owner of a business would sit down with a prospective employee and they would talk about the job that needed to be done. Maybe the employer was a blacksmith. Maybe he was a banker. The employer would ask around, "Does this guy do good work? Is he smart? Can he be counted on?" The boss invited the worker to show off his skills and to display samples of his work. If the boss was favorably impressed with the worker's capabilities and felt he would be a good asset to the business, the boss offered him the job. They would negotiate a little, maybe over the pay; maybe the worker needed some extra training; or maybe it was about the specific work to be done. The employer and the employee worked it out between them and came to an agreement. The entire procedure was one-on-one. The only things that mattered were: "Can this guy do the job?" "Is this the right job for me?" and "Can we agree on the pay?"

Then America began to industrialize. Companies grew at an amazing rate; the need for workers exploded. In many industries, companies were so profitable that they could afford to hire less discriminatingly. It was not difficult to replace workers. The Depression exacerbated this situation.

Soon employees could be hired right off the street. The boss sent out a weathered old truck every morning at 5 A.M. The truck drove around town, through the dark backstreets where men waited on corners. A foreman stood on the running board, and when the truck stopped he looked at the laborers and pointed to this one, this one, and that one. They climbed onto the flatbed and joined the others. When the foreman had enough laborers for that day's work, the truck drove back to the factory.

One day, the boss decided he had hired one too many people off the street. They just weren't working out. There was no way to tell whether a man would do a good job. Some were weak; others weren't smart enough or diligent enough. The boss had to find a way to evaluate a person before hiring him.

The interview was born.

As the economy grew and employers needed to hire more and more people, the search for workers became a little more complex. A manager advertised for qualified people to come in for interviews. When the number of responses became too large, employers couldn't meet everyone in person, so they asked for information in writing.

The résumé was born.

Employers culled the best candidates from the stacks of résumés, but there were still too many to evaluate. Special departments were formed to further sort through candidates before the boss met any of them. Soon companies hired outside experts to help them sort through even more paperwork and more job candidates.

The *employment industry* was born.

The hiring process became a huge, expensive enterprise called personnel and human resources. Every company of any size had people, processes, procedures, and rules to help them define jobs and evaluate job hunters.

The boss and the job applicant drifted farther and farther away from one another. Enormous amounts of time and resources were spent before these two ever met to talk about the job. That is, *if* they ever got to meet and talk. The number of personnel workers and the amount of paper that came between the boss and the applicant grew to ridiculous proportions.*

Sometimes, an applicant would lose interest in a company because an inexperienced personnel representative made the company and the job seem undesirable. Or, an applicant was declined because a representative of the company who knew little about the job decided the applicant did not fit the "profile" for the position.

The task of selecting workers turned into an institutionalized and error-prone shuffle of paper and people. The process got way out of hand. And now, it has ballooned into a major problem affecting the current job market. Perhaps that's why it's called a market. It's like an open-air free-for-all where everyone is trying to get a deal. Workers and jobs are represented as commodities. It almost doesn't matter what you "buy." What matters is that you're in the market, taking your chances with millions of other people. This is why traditional interviews are the wrong way to win a job, and the wrong way to hire a worker.

In today's world, trying to get interviews will ensure one thing: you will become one of the millions of people who are expending their energy getting processed, talking to personnel jockeys, getting disgusted, getting turned down, or getting hired into the

---

*Imagine if job hunters used the same approach as employers. You wouldn't have to go on an interview until the actual hiring manager was ready to meet you. Instead, you would first send a professional job hunter to interview with the company's employment agency, then with the company's professional candidate screener, then with the professional personnel representative. Your job hunter would tell them all about you and try to explain what kind of work you were good at performing. He would try to answer questions he wasn't really qualified to answer; but then again, the personnel professionals aren't really qualified to ask questions about how drugs are synthesized or how computers are programmed or how to sell more widgets to new customers. If your job hunter was favorably impressed with the opportunity, he would report back to you, and you would then decide whether to meet the manager who actually had an open job. Maybe you would send out a postcard that said "I'll get back to you." Wouldn't it be interesting if you could shop for a job the way companies shop for workers—without involving the decision maker (you) until very late in the "process"?

wrong job and then having to do it all over again because the job they got is not the job that's right for them.

Are so many millions of people wrong? Are employers so aloof that they choose to waste their time with this process? The answer, in too many cases, is yes. People and companies waste their time because they have bought into a system that has become dysfunctional; it focuses more on a process than on the worker and the work. This problem has insidiously crept up on our economy, and it is creating a gargantuan obstacle in an already troubled job market.

In a different day and age, going on interviews was actually a good way to find a job. Today, people sometimes go on literally dozens of interviews before they earn the reward they seek: a new job. This interviewing behavior doesn't really work very well—just ask someone who's been on his fifteenth interview. But this is how American workers have been trained to pursue a new job. If people think they will receive a reward at some point, they will engage in the most outrageous, useless behaviors—like interviewing.

WORKSHEET 2: DOES THE HIRING SYSTEM WORK?

The way the system supposedly works is that you send out résumés, get invited to interviews, get some job offers, and accept a job. Let's take a look at whether it really works. Pick a few of your relatives, friends, and business associates who have looked for a job in the past twelve months. In the boxes below, fill in the name of the person, the number of résumés he or she sent out, the number of interviews attended, and the number of offers received. For your conclusions to be appropriate, your figures must be accurate.

To see how well the résumés produced interviews, and how often the interviews yielded job offers, use two ratios: number of interviews attended divided by number of résumés sent out (interview ratio), and number of job offers divided by number of interviews attended (offer ratio). In a perfect world, the interview and offer ratios would divide out to 1.00; in other words, every résumé would produce an interview and every interview would yield an offer.

Person	# Résumés	# Interviews	# Offers	Interview Ratio	Offer Ratio

You must decide for yourself how many offers should reasonably result from a job hunter's efforts. Are you surprised at the ratios calculated from these real-life experiences?

Finally, ask two more questions for which we did not collect data. How many of the offers were accepted? And, how many of the people are now working at the jobs they accepted?

If you really want to have some fun, take a ratio of number of offers divided by number of résumés. The real shocker would be for an employer to take this same ratio: how many résumés did he receive for each job offer he extended?

Does the system work, in your opinion? Do résumé sending and interviewing seem to be productive behaviors when you are trying to find the right new job?

Don't Be a Pigeon

Let me illustrate why perfectly intelligent people engage in completely unsound behaviors. Many years ago, B. F. Skinner, the foremost behavioral scientist of our time, shed light on a phenomenon that seems more clear to us now.

Skinner put a hungry pigeon in a box that had a lever and a food trough in it. Pressing the lever made food roll down a tube and into the trough where the pigeon could get it. The pigeon wandered around in the box until it eventually pecked at the lever. Out came a food pellet, which the hungry pigeon ate. Later, the pigeon hit the lever again and more food was dispensed. Pretty soon the pigeon figured out the system and pecked at the lever whenever it wanted food. This is called *conditioning*. The pigeon continued to peck at the lever because this behavior was associated with food.

This was a great system for the hungry pigeon, until Skinner disconnected the food tube from the lever. Now the poor pigeon could peck at the lever for hours, but no food would come out. Every now and then, Skinner reconnected the tube. Now the pigeon got its reward at random times. The bird's pecking behavior no longer controlled whether food came down the tube. But the pigeon continued to peck away.

Skinner discovered that he could keep pigeons pecking essentially until they dropped dead of hunger. The birds acted as if they had learned something, when in fact they were just wasting their time. Call it conditioning, call it habit, or call it getting conned. The system stopped working because things were going on behind the scenes that the pigeons knew nothing about. But they kept pecking away, because now and then they got a reward. Their behavior was conditioned.

Does this mean the pigeons were stupid? Not at all. Skinner was able to show in other studies that pigeons are actually capable of learning pretty sophisticated things. What his work suggested was that perhaps animals—including people—are sometimes controlled more by *behaviors they learn* than by their intelligence.

In the past, interviewing was a simple, effective process that focused on the boss, the worker, and the job. Today, by the time you get to meet and talk with the boss, both you and he will be so worn out and distracted by this entire process that you probably won't really talk about forming a relationship to do a job.

I regularly see the consequences of this problem. Most job applicants will complete an interview without ever clearly expressing their desire for the job. Almost as often, they will not even ask about the details of the job for which they are interviewing. And the interviewer will act comparably, often failing to accurately describe the work or to adequately assess the candidate's ability to do it.

The outcome of this interview behavior is that the employer and the job hunter fail to accomplish what they set out to do: come together to do a job. The consequence of such dysfunctional interviews is that workers interview for too many jobs before they are hired, and companies waste time with innumerable candidates before making a hiring decision. The candidate and employer just keep pecking blindly at that interview lever, until a reward (in the form of a job or a worker) falls out of the sky.

Like Skinner's pigeons, the people involved have been conditioned to continue acting in a manner that no longer yields a reward. They focus more on the process than the outcome, more on the lever than the true source of the food, more on the interview than on the job.

Don't be a pigeon. Pigeons will keep pressing a lever long after it ceases to yield a reward. Their single occupation becomes pressing that lever, no matter what.

"Well," you might say, "people aren't pigeons. You can't condition people to behave like that. People know there's someone behind the scenes filling a hopper with food pellets. They know the lever doesn't produce the food. It's more complicated. The same is true when you're looking for a job. The interview process is just a necessary step, it's what you have to do to reach your real goal."

Years of interviewing people both as a headhunter and as an employer tell me just the opposite. People are willing to waste their time because they believe that's how the system works, and they superstitiously fear that if they don't follow the rules, they will be rejected. American business and American workers have bought into this dysfunctional system lock, stock, and barrel. It's so bad that interviewing has become a business: the interview, not the job it is supposed to yield, is the focus of attention.

Take a look in your favorite bookstore. You'll find more books on the shelves about *interviewing* and *job hunting* than books about how to perform a particular kind of job.* I don't know about you, but if I were hiring workers, I'd rather meet with someone who spent more time studying up on his work skills than reading about the latest interviewing techniques. I don't want to hire someone with flash; I want to hire someone with substance.

Workers are going on interviews for the sake of going on interviews. Job hunters interview without knowing anything about the job, the company, or the problems the employer needs solved other than what they read in a want ad. They then expect to be given a job because they sat and answered questions, not because they arrived at the interview with some well-thought-out solutions to the employer's problems.

"But," you might counter, "I go on an interview to find out about the job, and so the interviewer can find out about me."

The next time your boss asks you to meet with him to discuss a new project, are you going to sit like a bump on a log and wait for him to figure out whether you have the smarts to do the work? Or, are you going to take the initiative and *show him* how you are going to get this project done on time and within budget?

Are you going to act like someone off the street who has no idea how to tackle the project? Or, are you going to act like a trusted employee who has done his homework and is ready to take this project off the manager's hands?

---

*Am I adding to the clutter of such books? When you finish *Ask the Headhunter*, I think you will agree that the personnel jockeys who write books on this topic would rather gag on a broom handle than put this book in the same category as theirs.

Now ask yourself why you would do anything different for a meeting with your *future* boss to discuss a new job with his company. Forget about pecking at the interview lever. Instead, think about your work. Think about the job. Think about what you can do for your next employer.

WORKSHEET 3: THE INTERVIEW OR THE JOB?

What are you doing to find your next job? Are you blindly pecking at the interview lever, or are you focused on finding the one job that's right for you?

If you're not sure whether you are looking for the right job, you need help defining the job you want. Often, a good place to start is with the job you have. Write out your responses to the following exercises. The results will help you keep an eye on what you really want.

1. **What** • Describe the job you would want to be promoted to at your current (or last) company. Be honest with yourself, and be realistic. But let yourself dream about what you really want to do next. List the title, salary, responsibilities, and level of authority. What are the three most important goals you would have to achieve in that job, to be successful? What are the daily tasks you would be expected to perform?

2. **How** • How would you do this job if you had it? List the things you would need to do to achieve each of the three goals you described above. How would you perform the day-to-day tasks better than they are being performed now?

3. **Why** • Why should you be assigned this job? What profit would you add to your company's bottom line if you accomplished your goals? Make your best estimate. If you need to do some thinking and research to figure this out, do it. The profitability question is at the heart of every hiring decision.

If you're not satisfied with what you came up with, select another job and do the exercise again. Keep practicing until you feel good about the work and the job you want to do.

4. Review your plan with someone you respect and trust at the company, or with someone who understands your business. You may even be able to review it with your boss, explaining that this is your professional goal over the next year. Ask for suggestions to improve it. Listen carefully to all comments. (If you think this exercise might land you a promotion at your current

company, you're right. The same planning that will net you a new job else-where should work with your employer too.)

Now, use what you've learned here to define the job you want to find. Do not interview for jobs that fail to meet or exceed these requirements. Why waste your time settling for anything less?

Once you have identified the right job, you cannot be as powerful a candidate for any other job. In fact, you will fall on your face interviewing for other jobs, because they are not the job you want and are ready to do. Don't go after inter-views—go after the right job.

Interviews Are Not Jobs

Going on interviews is a lot like going on a diet. Once you start doing it, you keep doing it, even though the goal seems elusive. Soon you forget about really losing that weight. "Maybe I'm not taking all the weight off but, hey, at least I'm trying." Staying on the diet becomes the goal. So it is with interviews. Maybe you haven't found a job, but you're doing all the interviews you can. After a while, your real focus is on interviews. Getting them and doing them. You send out dozens or hundreds of résumés to get as many interviews as possible. You respond to dozens of ads, to get more interviews.

But interviews are not the objective, any more than dieting is. It's easy to get lost or sidetracked on the way toward your goal. Don't let that happen in your job search. Don't work harder at getting interviews than at winning a job. Here are a few ideas to guide you.

1. The goal is the right job, not more interviews.

Even the smartest people lose sight of this distinction once they are in the throes of their job search. Not long ago a neighbor referred someone to me. Tom is a manager with a major insurance company who had sixty days to find a new job due to a "reduction in force" at his company. He was having a very difficult time, he explained. He believed there just weren't many jobs available at his level of management. I agreed with him.

What was he doing about finding a new job, I asked. He had been on six interviews in the past ten days. None of them were panning out. Could I help him get more interviews? It was the classic case of a job seeker focused on getting interviews, rather than on finding the right job.

Tom couldn't understand what was wrong. He was doing what you're *supposed* to do when you look for a new job: he was lining up interviews. He had sent out many résumés and each day he set aside two hours to send out more. He was trying to keep the ball rolling and talk to as many people as possible. And yet, by his own admission, he was at a management level where there were just not that many jobs available. So, how could he possibly have found six *right* jobs to interview for in just ten days?

The answer was: he hadn't. He had found six *interviews* to go on. None of the jobs were quite right for him. But he felt he was accomplishing something because at least he was going out on interviews. Maybe he thought it was good practice. He knew that he was going to get turned down many times before he would get a job offer, and he accepted that. It seemed like he was trying to get as many rejections behind him as he could, as though that would improve his chances on subsequent interviews. Nothing could be farther from the truth.

He was pecking at the interview lever, and he was going to keep pecking at it no matter what.

Tom thought I might be able to help him. But when he spoke to me, he didn't bother to say much about his skills or work experience until I asked. Can you imagine that? His skills were the last thing on his mind. He was more concerned about where he was going to get his next interview.

He was running scared, and it was costing him dearly. Tom had become detached from his work, his abilities, and what he had to offer an employer. All he wanted to talk about was his new vocation: getting and doing interviews. Personnel departments love guys like Tom. He does what he's told: sends out résumés, waits, and comes when he's called.

Tom's experience is common. He caught *interview-itis* from an industry that tries to convince people that getting and doing interviews is a legitimate, full-time job in itself. It's not.

2. *Avoid interview-itis.*

The employment industry centers around finding and doing interviews, and only indirectly does it address a person's abilities or an employer's job needs. The employment industry is made up of personnel jockeys: career counselors, self-appointed job hunting experts (usually former personnel managers), human resources professionals, outplacement experts (more former personnel managers), in-house recruiters, employment agencies (including the government's), and résumé shops, to list a few.

All these "resources" have evolved to help you do the job of finding a job. They will teach you how to do it, and how to spend as much of your time as possible doing it. They will make it your new career. Their mission is helping you to go on as many interviews as possible, and then to schedule more.

Pow! You've got interview-itis.

The success of personnel jockeys depends on your catching this affliction. Once you catch it, they offer you the cure: more résumés, more interviews, more advice about résumés and interviews. The terminal form of interview-itis is when you start to act like doing interviews *is your job.*

Doing interviews *is not your job.* Doing interviews *is their job.* Don't let anyone confuse you.

How do you know whether you've contracted interview-itis? Look at how you're spending your time. If you are spending most of your time responding to ads, sending out résumés, going on interviews, and talking to personnel jockeys, you've got interview-itis. Better get over it quickly.

WORKSHEET 4: HAVE YOU GOT INTERVIEW-ITIS?

Score 10° F. for each symptom you have. If your temperature is above 100° F., you've got it.

SYMPTOMS OF INTERVIEW-ITIS

Check if you:

_____ Always scan the want ads in whatever newspaper you're reading

_____ Send out more than three résumés per week

_____ Send more résumés to personnel departments than to actual hiring managers

_____ Never sent a résumé to an actual hiring manager

_____ Saw an ad for the perfect job and are very excited about it

_____ Sent a résumé in response to a blind ad (no company name listed in the ad)

_____ Interviewed with personnel before meeting with the hiring manager

_____ Spent more time meeting with personnel than with the manager

_____ Never met with the hiring manager

_____ Knew more about the job than the personnel representative did

_____ Didn't know the hiring manager's name until personnel told you

_____ Filled out more than one form when meeting with personnel

_____ Called personnel to follow up after you met with the manager (rather than calling the manager)

_____ Were told by the personnel representative to please not call them, they will call you

_____ Got a card or form letter from a personnel representative saying "we received your résumé"

_____ Were told by personnel, rather than the hiring manager, that you're not qualified

_____ Interviewed with the hiring manager but never heard another word from him

_____ Have been on more than two interviews in a week

_____ Have been on more than five interviews total and still don't have any job offers

_____ Memorized the answers to the "top ten" interview questions

_____ Registered with more than one employment agency

_____ Sent your résumé to the same employer more than once in a six-month period

_____ Were told by personnel that the company is not presently hiring

_____ Sent your résumé to an employment agency that said it wasn't necessary to meet you

_____ Were told by the agency that they would send your résumé to dozens of employers

_____ Filled out a form from which a résumé shop created your résumé

_____ Had your résumé printed on colored paper stock

_____ Paid a career counselor a lot of money to learn how to "network yourself"

3. Dodging the personnel affliction.

Experts in the employment industry know little if anything about the work you do. Their training is in personnel administration. So, they spend all their time getting you to focus on the work *they* do: filling out forms, checking off buzzwords that describe your skills, evaluating your résumé, reviewing salary history, listing references, talking about employment regulations, discussing benefits, waiting until they interview internal candidates, calculating how long you had your last job, and so on. As far as they are concerned, personnel is a science unto itself. That's what they specialize in. The work you do is almost irrelevant to them.

That's why human resources people can work one day for an insurance company and the next for a chemical company. That's why an employment agency places secretaries one minute, production workers the next hour, and computer programmers the day after. The job does not matter; the *job description* does. Its almost irrelevant to the personnel jockey how an applicant does a job, as long as the applicant fits the job description. (That's why computerized résumé scanning—perhaps the most shocking insult to job hunters and managers—is becoming so popular in personnel organizations. It helps personnel jockeys process résumés containing even more terminology that they don't understand.) The process matters most, and the process is a numbers game. If enough applicants can be crammed into the process, one or two good ones will eventually come out. The less accurate the personnel jockey is, the more applicants he has to process. This creates more work for him, and that makes his job secure.

Whether they do it consciously or not, personnel jockeys get you, the job hunter, to buy into this system because they convince you that they are in charge. They are the doctor. You are the patient. You should do as you're told, without asking too many questions. Just fill out this form, and answer all the questions that are fired at you. Take two aspirin, but don't call them in the morning. They'll call you. Next?

4. The truth about who does the hiring.

Time and again I hear human resources (HR) managers refer to the "thousands of people" they've hired—and how expert they are at the hiring process. In fact, HR managers don't hire anyone but other HR workers. Yet they'd have you believe you're going to be working for them, and that it's *them* you've got to impress.

Bunk.

These "experts" have become a part of the infrastructure that daily distracts you from the all-important goal of your job search: the job. Personnel jockeys encourage you to read all the ads, contribute to the mass of résumés in companies' filing cabinets, and wait for their call. Finally, they "invite" you in to be paraded like cattle along with hundreds of other souls so they can interview you. They don't *want* you to talk to the hiring manager before they screen you. They want you green and they want you under control.

When was the last time a personnel jockey sent you a written job description before he interviewed you? He asked you for your résumé, didn't he? Isn't it a little odd that a company wants to know about you before the interview, but sees no reason to tell you much about the job or the person you would be working for, so you can prepare properly for your meeting?

> Any manager who is serious about hiring a good worker *wants a job candidate to know as much as possible about the job before the interview,* because he only wants to meet workers who are prepared and ready to do the job. But in most companies, managers are not supposed to communicate with candidates until well into the hiring process.

The manager's initial contribution to candidate selection is to fill out a job description form and submit it to a personnel jockey. But that piece of paper will never make it into the hands of the candidate, either before or after the interview. In many cases, the job description is "company confidential." Who do you think is interested in hiding that job description? Not the hiring manager!

This may sound like quite an attack on America's employment industry. Well, it is an attack. Very few personnel jockeys care as much about you and the job as the hiring manager does. The inappropriate—and often meaningless—disapproval of a personnel jockey can cost you your job hunting sanity, and it can cost an employer the opportunity to hire a wonderful worker.

A reader of my *Ask the Headhunter* forum on America Online recently shared his disheartening story of rejection. A health problem forced him to stop working for a while, but he used this time to actually improve his work skills. Healthy again and eager to work, he reported on his experiences.

I have kept current with my skills and knowledge (I am seeking an administrative assistant/sales assistant position with a brokerage firm) and have expanded on them, and emphasize this during the interview. At every interview I have been to thus far, though, I still am informed that my employment gap is "a serious problem." I have even brought examples of my at-home work, to no avail.

I had only one question for this dejected rejectee: Who were these people who were telling you, in essence, that they'd never hire you?

The people telling me that my "gap" was a problem were personnel, not the ones who would make the final hiring decision (or, for that matter, the ones who would be working with me).

What happened when he cut the personnel folks out of the picture?

On the two interviews I've had where I went directly to the person who was doing the hiring, my hiatus was only briefly mentioned in the context of "and what skills do you have now?" types of questions.

The impact this "human resources" profession has on your ability to find a new job is immense. Sit up and take notice; understand how the employment industry affects you. *The employment industry does not hire anyone, except of course, other personnel jockeys.*

5. *Vital work skills vs. irrelevant job seeking skills.*

Think about this carefully. Personnel jockeys make a living helping companies fill jobs, but they know next to nothing about the jobs they fill. There is something very wrong here that permeates every aspect of job hunting, from classified ads to employment agencies to the way employers force you to meet with their personnel departments before you talk with the manager who's going to hire you. The "job" has gotten lost in this great infrastructure.

In recent years, "job seeking skills" seem to have become as important as actual work skills. The personnel jockeys have built a moat around corporate America, and they pretend to control the drawbridge. They prefer that you jump into the mucky moat itself and duke it out with them first. In fact, for a fee, career counselors and adult education courses will teach you the job seeking skills they dictate you must use.

But these skills are spurious. If you learn them and practice them you will get stuck deeper in the moat. You will develop interview-itis and start to believe that the personnel jockeys are the people with whom you have to get interviews. This will distract you from talking to the one person who really controls the drawbridge: the manager who needs to hire you.

Six of the more popular "job seeking skills" actually reveal critical fallacies people succumb to when searching for work in today's job market:

1. It has become more important for a job seeker to read want ads than to identify the right companies to approach.

2. It has become more important to seek out go-betweens—recruiters, personnel managers, employment agencies, want ads, computerized job listings—than managers who have jobs.

3. It has become more important to know what to say to personnel recruiters—even though these recruiters know less about a company's business than the applicant himself knows—than to know what to say to the manager who has an actual job to fill.

4. It has become more important to have a résumé that describes you enticingly than to learn all you can about the job you are applying for.

5. Job hunters have learned to answer questions like "where do you see yourself in five years?" but it never occurs to them to be able to say "let me show you how I do this job."

6. It has become more important to prove to a personnel manager that you fit the job description than it is to demonstrate how a company might profit from hiring you.

These fallacies are prevalent not only among job hunters but also among employers. Job hunters complain about how many résumés they've mailed out and how many fruitless interviews they've had. Companies complain about how many résumés and interviews they have to wade through to find the right worker. Is it any wonder? If both parties would only do their homework, they could find one another without so much fuss.

If you have fallen prey to the misconceptions listed above, you have interview-itis. You are stuck in the moat. Neglecting to focus on your work skills will have a devastating impact on your job search. You will find yourself waiting for the employment industry to pluck you out from among millions of others who are sinking around you.

While you wait, no company will tell you whether it is seriously considering hiring you or why it has not made a decision. Worse, you might get a little postcard, which no one has bothered to sign, that reads:

Other candidates have been identified who are more suitable to this job, but your résumé will be kept on file in the event our needs change. Your qualifications are admirable and we are certain you will find a suitable position, somewhere at the bottom of the moat, like sucking rocks.

In spite of all the information they've collected from you, they still can't tell you exactly why they're not hiring you. Odds are pretty good that they don't really know why. That's because they don't know whether you can do the job, or how you might benefit their business. They didn't ask. You didn't tell them. So you're out there, swimming in circles around the moat.

Why does everyone waste their time? In a bizarre sort of way, the process works because it is a numbers game and eventually (if you can wait that long) a number will come up (although it may not be *your* number). The system just doesn't work the way you need it to. But you have more control over it than you may suspect.

To get out of the moat, you have to make use of your *work skills*. This, after all, is what an employer will ultimately pay you for. In fact, your work skills are all you need to get safely over this troll-infested moat to talk to the hiring manager. Work skills include the expertise and knowledge you use to meet your professional responsibilities. Work skills refer to your mastery of the tools you actually use every day to exert your creative power over the tasks your employer needs you to accomplish. Your abilities, your talents, your proficiency at meeting challenges in your work: that's what wins a job offer. This is what the manager who's going to hire you wants to know about.

When you walk into an interview, it has to be for a job that you carefully selected—a job that you are ready and able to do. You have to take responsibility for controlling the interview, and for helping the employer break out of the traditional interview process. You are not another "wannabe" candidate waiting for the employer to figure out whether you are worthy of the job. You are not there to be interrogated. You are there to solve the manager's problems. You are not there to do the interview. You are there to do the job.

WORKSHEET 5: ARE YOU STUCK IN THE HIRING MOAT?

Take a slice of time, for example, the last three months, and compare the ways you spent your time. Fill in the #Hrs and # columns for each item below and total each section up.

A Hours you spend:	#Hrs	B Vs. hours you spend:	#Hrs
Reading want ads		Researching target companies	
Talking on the phone to personnel jockeys		Talking on the phone to managers who can hire you	
Meeting with personnel jockeys		Meeting with hiring managers	
Preparing your résumé		Researching the next job you will interview for	
Studying job hunting books & memorizing answers to typical interview questions		Studying your job & deciding how best to demonstrate how you do your work	
Waiting to hear back from a company about a job		Answering the Four Questions about that job	
A Total		B Total	

C Number of:	#	D Vs. number of:	#
Personnel jockeys you have talked with on the phone		Hiring mangers you have talked with on the phone	
Personnel jockeys with whom you have met		Hiring managers with whom you have met	
Résumés you have mailed		Responses you have received	
Meaningless questions you've answered in interviews		Times you've *demonstrated* your skills in interviews	
Personnel jockeys who asked you how many years' experience you have		Personnel jockeys who really understood the work you do or how you could add to the profit line	
Times you were rejected after submitting your résumé or being interviewed		Times you were told, clearly and explicitly, why you were being rejected	
Interviews you have gone on		Offers you have received	
C Total		*D Total*	
Add A + C		*Add B + D*	

If B + D is greater than A + C, you have cleared the moat and you're moving in the right direction. If A + C is the larger score, you're stuck in the moat mud; the personnel jockeys are pulling you under. Grab for a rope!

Beating the Failed Methods of the Employment System

There is an enormous distinction between "doing work" and "having a job." There is likewise a distinction between hiring the right person to do work and filling a job. The employment system is not geared toward hiring anyone to accomplish work that needs to be done. Only an actual hiring manager can do such hiring. When a bureaucratic infrastructure gets in the way, all a company can do is fill jobs. The infrastructure simply does not know the work the way the manager and the worker know it. As a result, the wrong people are hired altogether too often, and some of the best people for a job *don't* get hired.

The system is dumb. It follows a simpleminded set of rules that, as a job hunter, you can easily beat. Headhunters do it all the time, and employers gladly pay them to do it. Like a head-hunter, you can cut to the core of what hiring is all about: helping the employer be more successful by doing what you do best—profitable work. When you can do this, the system can't touch you. I've placed many people in companies where the personnel organization had a policy against using headhunters. I was able to do it not because I was a good salesman—the personnel department never even knew I was there—but because individual hiring managers needed my help. They need your help, too. Just make sure what you're offering is help—and that you're not wasting their time.

1. Take control of the interview.

Carefully select the right companies, the right managers, and the right jobs. Talk only to the manager who needs to hear what you have to say. If you're ready to walk in the door and be expert at solving a manager's problems, then he'll always be ready to talk to you. You will never have to impress a personnel jockey again.

56

2. Master your attitude.

Don't be someone standing lamely in line waiting for a job, amidst competitors who have no idea what the employer really needs. Be ready to act like an employee by demonstrating your ability to do the work.

3. Master the information.

No one will prepare you to perform this compelling demonstration. You've got to do it on your own. You must gather and master the information you'll need to solve the problems the employer is facing. For every personnel jockey who doesn't understand the work you do, there's a hiring manager who cares about nothing *but* the work you do. Be totally prepared to address this manager. Have something valuable to say and be ready to follow up with that demonstration.

4. Do the job to win the job.

In essence, you are tackling a project as you do on any job. You must impress the employer just as you would want to impress your boss—with your ability to deliver, to *do the job.*

This is how the headhunter coaches your competition for the job. Are you ready?

CHAPTER 4

Take Control of the Interview

Don't Stand in Line

Let's blame Henry Ford for creating the quandary that job hunters find themselves in today. It was Ford, after all, who perfected the production line.

Replacement parts for cars used to be handmade to fit, until Henry started manufacturing all piston rods to be exactly the same. All door handles were exactly alike. Everything that was replaceable became standard, so that it could be manufactured in great quantities on production lines. This process made car parts readily available. It was another kind of numbers game—except in this numbers game, every part of a type was exactly like every other one.

Perhaps at some point America started to believe that its workers and managers were just as replaceable, and just as easy to come by, as mass-produced parts. So corporate America invented a sort of personnel production line: line them up, interview them, pick out the ones that fit, and send them on up to management for final inspection and installation.

The problem is, not all workers are alike. *They don't all fit.* In America's rush to do more and do it faster, business has started treating people like interchangeable parts. The employment industry has been geared to mold you so you will fit into the standard hiring process.

A personnel department sees things this way because it has to process many new employees. But as jobs become more and more specialized today, a manager knows the value of the "handmade" job candidate. The manager isn't looking for standard parts. He wants someone from a special mold who can make his department work better and more profitably.

The manager who's going to hire you might go along with this numbers game because he figures that at some point the worker he needs will appear on the hiring line. He desperately wants the next candidate who rolls in to be the last he'll have to interview. He has a job that needs to be done, and he wants to get back to work himself.

If you approach your job interviews in the right way, you can take control of them and actually help the hiring manager in the process. Here are ten ways to avoid standing on the hiring line with your competitors.

1. Stop doing what everyone else is doing.

Stop worrying about responding to all the want ads. If you carefully consider what happens when you rely on ads, you'll realize that you're throwing yourself into a sea of competition. The sheer volume of responses a company gets when it places a job ad proves this. You're actually putting yourself at a disadvantage by willingly competing with so many job candidates.

Stop thinking about interviews and about what questions you're going to be asked. Don't turn into an interview junkie. The typical job candidate worries more about how he's going to perform in the interview than about whether—or how—he can do the job. It never ceases to amaze me how little people know about a job they are interviewing for. And it shows. That's why most job hunters leave the interview wondering what—if anything—is going to happen next. The answer is: nothing. The employer can smell an interview junkie a mile away. Ultimately, interview junkies all work for the employment industry. If you can avoid becoming one, you'll never have to compete with them again.

2. Start thinking about the work you do.

When we were kids, the teacher used to startle us when we were daydreaming by calling out, "Johnny! The answer isn't out the window!" Something was distracting us from our lessons and taking us away from the challenge at hand. It's impossible to focus on your job search if you let your mind start wandering over all those possible jobs. The easiest way to get lost is to go off in fifty directions at once by applying for every job that seems related to the work you do. *The work you do.* Remember that? Think long and hard about it, because it's the only thing you can talk to an employer about that will actually help you win an offer. If you lose your focus, you'll flap around in the interview like a fish out of water. I have met precious few people who are good at talking about their work in an interview. Most are too busy trying to psych out the interviewer. But if you think more about your work, you'll find new ways to impress an employer.

3. Live with the natives.

The best workers strive to understand all they can about the business in which they work. They associate with colleagues, so that they can learn more about their field and expand their expertise. They are members of a professional community. Try to spend your time with people who are happy and successful at the kind of work you want to do. This is the best way to get close to your target job. You will learn things (including where to find such jobs) that are inaccessible to outsiders. Focus on more than just finding your next job: investigate companies and get to know people who do the work you want to do, *before* you need a new job. Your competitors' résumés may wind up in some personnel jockey's drawer, but your new friends will take you into the inner sanctum of the hiring manager.

4. Become an expert.

How well do you really know the industry you want to work in? Are you current on new ideas and how they are being applied? Do you have any good ideas of your own to bring to the table? Instead of trying to submit a fancier résumé than the next guy, take a little time to fill holes in your knowledge and sharpen your skills. Become an expert at what you do. Then share your expertise with others in your field—that's how you become even more expert and gain recognition.

When a headhunter seeks out a good candidate for one of his clients, he looks among his quarry's professional associates. He looks for the one person everyone else is talking about. Will he find you? This is not to say that you should "play to the head-hunter." However, positioning yourself properly in your field will make you more visible to headhunters, to lots of employers, and to the managers who work for them.

5. Learn to show, not just tell.

Learn to demonstrate your abilities, not just talk about them. Remember that your goal is to help an employer solve his problems and meet his challenges. Any candidate is ready to tell a story or two in an interview. You know the standard prattle: "When I was back there in military school, we parked the commanding officer's Cadillac up on the roof of the gym. I was a pretty clever guy." Or, "Well, yes, I once closed a six-zillion-dollar deal when I found a way to help a customer lease the equipment with nothing down. They named me Employee of the Year for that. Impressive, huh?"

Your abilities are not dead heroes buried beneath your old employer's building. They are vital, living tools that you bring with you to the interview. And they need air! Why tell stories about them? Let them out! Don't tell the interviewer what you've done. *Show* him what you can do today, for *his* company.

I recently worked with a woman who wanted a top-level management job with a clothing retailer. Lynn was at a very challenging point in her life—recently divorced, with two children and lots of bills to pay. She couldn't afford to stand in line waiting for someone to recognize her abilities. Quite simply, her situation had forced her to take stock of her own value and to take a very pragmatic approach to her job search. She realized that if she could only get an employer to *see* what she could do, they would hire her. She used the Four Questions to get herself off the hiring line.

Lynn knew she was one of many talented candidates for a better-paying job. In the middle of the interview, she stood up and walked to the door. "Come on," she announced to the manager who was interviewing her, as she led him onto the selling floor. "I'm going to show you what I can do." And she proceeded to work the floor for half an hour, with the manager in tow. He made her an offer right there in the middle of the store.

Turn your interview into a meeting between two people who share a goal and who are motivated to explore how they can work together to get a job done in the best way possible. Approach your interview as an opportunity to solve problems and demonstrate your skills. Spend your next interview doing your job in the company of someone with whom you may decide to work for the next several years.

---

6. Get off the hiring line—get into the work.

A college student I know needed to earn money for Christmas gifts. A local factory was advertising for temporary production workers. Van went to the mass "interview" and stood in line with several dozen other students. The shift foreman was randomly selecting workers. (As production workers, all college students are equal, right?) You could almost hear the recruits thinking out loud: "Pick me! Pick me!"

As he made his selections, the foreman handed each new hire a time card with either a red or a blue stripe on it. Van nudged another company representative who was standing nearby. "What's the difference between red and blue?" "Blue is for material handlers. They get paid more." By this time the foreman was cursing because he was out of blue cards.

Van stepped off the line and walked up to the foreman. "You need more material handlers?" The foreman reacted as though a cow had broken herd and walked up to ask the time. "Yeah, I need more material handlers," he growled, fingering the red-striped cards. Van reached out and took a blue marker from the boss's shirt pocket, plucked a card out of his hand, and drew a blue stripe through the red one. "You're in luck. I'm a material handler," Van said. The foreman looked Van up and down and replied, "Then get to work."

Find your own way to step off that hiring line.

7. Learn to establish your value.

The Four Questions are your way off the hiring line. Any good job will require more preparation than Van had to do. But Van essentially answered the Four Questions—he quickly assessed the nature of the work, his ability to do it, and the manager's need. Then he stepped off the hiring line to distinguish himself from his competition, and showed the manager how to solve his immediate problem. Van took a risk, but he proved beyond doubt that he was ready to tackle the work that needed to be done.

Here's the main prescription of this book again, but in new terms. Instead of thinking about how to do interviews, think about:

1. What exactly is the work I do (or want to do), and how do I apply my skills to it?
2. What work does a specific employer need to have done? How does it fit in with my skills? How would I do that work?
3. How would I communicate the way I would do the work to the prospective employer? How would I demonstrate it?
4. How would I enable the employer to profit from my doing the job?

Compare these questions to the Four Questions. The questions above focus on you rather than on the job. Specifically, these questions help you define *the value you offer to an employer*. That gives you control in an interview.

8. Weed out the wrong jobs.

Think about the questions above for *every job opportunity* you consider. Gather the information you need to address each point thoroughly. After a while, you will be able to quickly weed out the wrong jobs, because you won't be willing to waste your time answering these questions about them. You'll get good at the process of elimination. You will avoid bad interviews. If you focus on jobs where you can offer your best, then you'll become the powerful answer to a specific employer's needs. And having something that someone needs gives you control like nothing else.

9. Talk to your grandmother.

You have no doubt walked out of an interview wondering, "What the heck was he talking about?" The jargon of an industry or business can be so thick you can't cut it with a chain saw. Employers aren't always clear about the nature of a job, or about the work they want done. But job candidates are often guilty of the same thing, especially if they're changing careers. They just can't clearly articulate what it is they're good at, or how they can be valuable to the employer. This leaves the employer cold—and it leaves the candidate without a job offer. Learn to be clear. Remember that others probably won't comprehend your abilities the way you do.

When you ask the Four Questions about a particular job, review your understanding with others. Learn to describe your work (or the job you're considering) so that your grandmother would understand it. Explain it *simply*. Practice describing how you do your job, or how you would do another one. Try to explain to a friend how a particular employer could profit from what you do. Be specific. If you can't explain it so that your grandmother will understand it, then you probably won't be able to explain it to an employer you've never met before in the limited context of an interview.

10. Stand out.

The candidate who is most attractive to an employer stands out from the rest. He "jumps off the hiring line" at the manager. This candidate takes it upon himself to define, for the manager's benefit, the value he is offering. What he has to say about the work he does is compelling and well thought out. It's clear from his professional affiliations that he is well regarded by his peers. If he's not an expert, he's on his way to becoming one.

The most powerful candidate for a job isn't the one who talks about his past glories; he's the one who offers to show how he can make the employer more successful here and now. There is no question that he understands what his role will be in contributing to the employer's profitability. He's not arrogant, but he assertively steps up and offers to take a load off the manager's back onto his own. He reveals the confidence of a person who has chosen this job because he's right for it. Most important, he communicates his value loud and clear: there's no question he has done his homework and that he's ready to hit the ground running.

Do you want to see a manager's eyes light up? His jaw drop? Then, in the interview, take control of the work he needs to have done, so that he can get on with his own job.

WORKSHEET 6: WHAT IS YOUR VALUE?

The Four Questions help you focus on what you can offer an employer. They also help you identify the kinds of jobs you want to pursue. The exercise below is derived from the Four Questions, and is heavily geared toward communicating your value to employers. To be able to do the job in an interview, you must be able to explain the work you do so that others will understand it. Your explanation must be clear and compelling.

Exercise: Your company's board of directors is planning the company's future, and the directors need to know what assets they have to work with. They need to know what their single employee does that attracts customers and makes money. Describe the work you do (include new things *you would like to do*) to help them plan for the future. The board has provided you with the questions below.

1. What is the product or service you produce? How good is it, compared to the competition? What makes it as good as it is? What must be done to improve it?

2. What goals does the company count on you to accomplish regarding this product or service? How do your skills qualify you to accomplish these goals?

3. If the board were to authorize you to hire a staff to do your work and ask you to manage that staff, what specific skills should the new employees possess?

4. The new staff will also need their own tools (you're keeping yours, just in case). What tools will you have to purchase for them? What new tools should you add to the arsenal? How would you get them trained to use these tools?

5. The new staff will have to perform all the tasks you now perform. How will you direct them, to ensure the continued success of the company? Show why these new employees won't cost more money than they produce for the company.

6. Create a report the new workers will submit to you each week, listing their goals, responsibilities, and achievements. This will let you decide which employees to keep, which to give bonuses to, which to promote, and which to fire.

7. Profits need to be higher. How can you change these jobs so it will cost less to do them? How can these jobs be changed to produce more revenue?

8. The board thinks you're doing a great job, but they're afraid you might get hit by a truck. They don't really understand what you do or how your work produces profit for the company. They want you to do a brief presentation to explain the business to them, so they'd be able to continue without you. Since your grandmother is on the board, and she doesn't understand much about business, they don't want to see anything too complicated. Use simple diagrams and drawings. Put your presentation together and practice it in front of a friend. Is your presentation good enough to present to the board? Will your grandmother understand it?

This exercise strengthens your Four Questions muscle. It reveals your value as an employer sees it. It helps you develop the ability to communicate your value in a compelling way.

The Shocking Truth:
Why Companies Conduct Interviews

Many job hunters think the purpose of an interview is to get a job. They could not be more wrong. Approaching an interview with this attitude will start you off at a disadvantage. There is a marked difference between people who are out to *get a job* and people who are out to *do a job.*

A person who is trying to get a job expects an employer to give him a job. Employers don't conduct interviews with the intent to give anyone anything. They conduct interviews to get a job done.

Build for yourself the attitude that you are out to do a job, not to be given one. A job is not something you acquire. It is something you do. Doing a job constitutes a valuable, self-motivated contribution to an employer's business. This attitude implies that you are not seeking just any job. You are seeking only one job: a job you can master and in which you can deliver value. An employer will pay handsomely for this attitude.

Companies interview people because they want to find a *specific* person. Every other candidate they see is a waste of their time. The candidate who proves he can do a specific job better than anyone else will likely be the one hired. It's easy to see who the company believes can do the job—he's the one the company is spending its money on.

And that brings us to the question, Is the interview conducted for the benefit of the employer or the candidate? To find the answer to this question, follow the money.

The employer is the one offering to pay a worker in exchange for his services. This means that the interview is conducted for the employer's benefit because he's the one spending money to get a job done. This buyer-seller distinction gives the employer some special privileges in the hiring process.

It is absolutely critical that you understand this point: *The immediate purpose of the interview is to benefit the employer.* The company's goal is to confirm whether a candidate can do the job, and this goal stands above the candidate's goal to ensure that this company and job are definitely right for him.

This statement will send some tempers flaring. After all, a worker has every right (indeed, a responsibility) to interview the company to make sure it's right for him. We have even said that a job hunter should be reasonably certain a job is right for him before he goes to the interview. During the interview, company and worker confirm the details that are important to each of them.

But the company's interests supersede the candidate's, at least at the outset of the interview. The candidate is selling, the company is buying. Until the company is sold on the candidate, the candidate is in no position to negotiate terms and conditions, *or even to confirm to himself that he definitely wants the job.*

As the host, the company starts the process with its job requirement, and its interests must be respected. The successful candidate will focus on the company's needs before he focuses on his own. He will respect the company's position of control by focusing on the job. *He will be ready to demonstrate that he can do the job to satisfy the company's needs.*

This initial control gives the employer huge power in the interview. What about the candidate's power? Does he have any?

As a candidate, you will eventually derive your power in the interview from the fact that you have satisfied the employer's needs. The best approach to the interview is to focus on what the company needs *because the first purpose of an interview is to enable the company to get the job done*, not for you to get a job. The candidate's own interest will be served best by waiting until after the company has decided it wants to hire him. Only then can the candidate truly "interview the company," decide whether he wants the job, and negotiate terms of employment.

If you approach interviewing with the company's needs firmly in mind, you will not only improve your chances of winning an offer, but also position yourself to take control of the interview at the appropriate moment. You will gain negotiating leverage that you will need later. You will use this leverage most effectively after the employer makes you an offer.

The Real Challenge of the Interview

As in sports, there are winners and losers in interviews. Only one person wins the job; many others who have applied lose. In sports there are games, and then there are *games*. When athletes perform at their peak and a game comes together perfectly, new marks are entered in the record books. That's the real challenge of any sport: to excel and achieve perfect performance.

The same is true in interviewing. Companies hire people every day. Sometimes, they hire the perfect candidate for the perfect job. That is the real challenge of interviewing.

Why aren't all hires perfect matches between job and candidate? Because most interviewers and candidates are distracted from the real challenge by wrongheaded rules that turn interviews into dull question-and-answer exchanges rather than what they should be: a dynamic opportunity for two people to work together.

> An interview is an exciting engagement between two people who share a common goal: to get a job done. They have the opportunity to take a fresh look at the work to be done and to explore the best way to do it.

The employer can stop and look at exactly what he wants done and how he wants it done. For him, the excitement and challenge lie in the possibility that he will find a worker who can bring a new vitality and talent to doing the job.

For the candidate, an interview is the opportunity to test his skills in front of an employer who really needs help. This is an opportunity to show a captive audience—the employer—the best way to do the job.

Therefore, the fundamental agenda of an interview has two parts. First, the employer must communicate the nature of the job that has to be done. This includes a description and an explanation of the work. The candidate should already know and understand these requirements from the research he did before the interview. Second, the candidate must demonstrate that:

- he understands the job that needs to be done;
- he can do the job;
- he can do the job the way the manager wants it done; and
- he can do the job profitably for the company.

The challenge is a perfect match between the job and the worker. The preparation required for this kind of exchange is significant. The candidate must know beforehand as much as possible about the job, about the manager, and about the company, and be confident that he can do the job profitably before he goes into the interview.

In the interview, it is incumbent upon the employer and the candidate to share and confirm their understandings about the job to be done, and about the candidate's ability to do it. The exchange regarding this topic must be thorough and it must be complete. *The interviewer and the candidate must confirm that the candidate can do the job.*

All the other "stuff" in an interview is secondary. This is not to say it isn't important. You have to be compatible with the employer, you have to be motivated, you have to indicate you're going to stick around, and you must fit with the rest of the team. (These issues are covered later in this book.) But if you say all the right things on these topics and can't convince the employer that you can *do the job*, the other "stuff" won't matter. While it may benefit a company to know the candidate's view of his future, his attitude about his old boss, his interest in sports, and his explanation about why he really wants this job, these are all secondary considerations in hiring a good worker.

Seize the Interview

Too often, no one questions the traditional interview process because no one really likes to do interviews—not the employer, and not the candidate. People smile and bear it because they just want to get it *over with*.

Few managers go to the trouble to walk a candidate through the place where the work is to be done, showing him the tools to be used and demonstrating what the job entails from start to finish. Few managers explain in hard, fast detail what their problem is and where they need help.

Likewise, few job candidates actually *show* an interviewer how they will do the work for which they are being considered. Instead, they sit passively fielding the manager's questions and encouraging the manager to wander off into a discussion about his golf game. It is a fatal mistake to think that by distracting the manager you're cleverly avoiding "the tough stuff."

Is it any wonder when a manager is surprised that a seemingly good interviewee has turned out to be a poor worker?

Personnel departments go on devising procedures to evaluate

job candidates, but almost all of these involve *talking* with the candidate; few of them involve talking in depth about the work; and almost no interview technique involves *doing the job*. So what is a good, prepared candidate to do? It is ultimately up to you to guide your interviews toward their critical purpose: proof that you can do the job.

Many hours wasted in interviews could be saved by putting a candidate in front of the job that needs to be done, letting him ask questions about it, and having him do it for a time. But companies rarely do this. And meek job candidates never volunteer to do the job because they are not prepared.

The Four Questions must be answered clearly and definitively during an interview. Once they are, the meeting can proceed any way the employer and the candidate want. The traditional format is not necessary. However, interviews cannot be reduced to all talk and no action. The interviewer's challenge is not to decide whether a candidate can do the job after only talking with him. The challenge is to find a candidate who can answer yes to the Four Questions. And the Four Questions cannot be answered without a compelling demonstration. They cannot be answered without the candidate *doing the job* during the interview.

When an interviewer fails to confirm whether you can do the job and do it exceptionally, he fails to meet the challenge of the interview. If this is the case in your interview, it is your responsibility to meet the challenge, both for yourself and for the employer. In other words, *you* must act: seize the interview.

Raise the ante for all other candidates and give yourself an edge by giving the interviewer the opportunity to hire a perfect candidate. Show the interviewer how to turn the interview into a demonstration of your abilities, proof that you can do the job. Let the interviewer benefit from all the research and homework you did in preparation for this job.

Meet the Employer's Needs

There is a lot of power in a meeting between a good worker and a good employer. It doesn't always get applied properly. In some cases, the power is never revealed during the meeting because neither the candidate nor the interviewer knows how to control the interview. But this power can make or break the meeting.

If you want an offer, you have to control the interview. You must rise up and reveal your power.

You may have heard it said that you should not draw a gun on someone unless you intend to kill him. In the martial arts, a student is taught to aim a punch at the far side of the object he's going to hit. That is, he is taught to punch clear *through* the object. The message in these instructions is, be thoroughly committed to your intention through your action. Leave nothing to chance or up to your opponent.

Never enter an interview without the intent and the means of controlling it. Never enter an interview without the intent and means of winning a job offer.*

Without such powerful intent, you will get creamed in an interview. If you take a lackadaisical attitude about your preparation or about the meeting, or if you are not sure you're interested in the job, don't go on the interview. If you are unprepared, you will have no power. The interviewer alone will control the interview. Or, worse, there will be no control in the interview. It will be a waste of time for you both. If you do not ultimately control the interview, you will not win a job offer.

How does a job candidate take control of an interview? *You make*

---

*Don't confuse this with accepting a job. Accepting a job is something you decide after the interview is over and you have an offer, and after you have done a follow-up interview of the company.

it your responsibility to ensure that the needs of the employer are met. Don't wait for him to do it, because if his needs are not met, he will blame you.

As soon as you have shown the employer that you are the person who can meet his needs, the power in the interview will tip in your direction, because you will have made him need you.

Ultimately, the act of doing the job in the interview gives you power because it reveals that you can satisfy the employer's needs. His challenge now is to hire you. If some of what follows sounds obvious, bear with me. Ideas that contain truth are usually simple and they *sound* correct. These ideas are often the most difficult to assimilate into the way we think because we are so accustomed to thinking another way.

Interviews did not become senseless and unproductive overnight. It took employment experts years to program us to waste one another's time by chasing inappropriate "opportunities." Creating a powerful approach to interviewing involves relearning some basic skills. In particular, it is important to understand the subtleties of how people communicate about the fundamental topic of working together as employer and employee.

The job is the only reason for a relationship between the worker and the employer. The interview is about the job, not about sitting and answering a bunch of questions correctly. And it is not about *getting* a job. It is about *doing* the job: *whether* and *how* you can work together with the employer to get it done the way he wants it done.

This brings us to a simple, straightforward strategy for interviewing that works. A candidate needs to accomplish four tasks to succeed in an interview:

1. *Prove* to the employer that you understand the job to be done.
2. *Demonstrate* that you can do the job.
3. *Demonstrate* that you can do the job the way the employer wants it done.
4. *Show* how the company will profit from hiring you.

It should be no surprise that these are "action tasks" related to the Four Questions. They will take you where you want to go: to the job. Just as important, they will help you take the employer with you. This strategy will give you control of the interview because it will help you satisfy the employer's need to find someone who can get the job done.

The rest of this book is devoted to teaching you how to accomplish these four tasks in your interviews.

Respect the Employer's Power . . . Then *Take Control*

Taking control of an interview will ultimately serve both your purpose and the employer's. Before you can take control, however, you must demonstrate your respect for the employer's power in the meeting. Let's look at how these two seemingly conflicting ideas come together in a good meeting.

Jack, a successful consultant who is a friend of mine, is fond of explaining how he approaches each assignment: "My client is in charge, but I am always in control." What Jack is saying is that his client, as the host of the relationship, has needs that dominate the relationship. The client hired the consultant, and the client is the one shelling out the money; therefore, the client is in charge.

Jack's value to the client lies in the fact that he takes responsibility for meeting the client's needs. In short, he does what he was brought in to do. Jack refers to this as having control in the relationship.

Now, we can argue about the fine points of what it means to be "in charge" and "in control." Jack's point is that there is power on both sides of a working relationship because the employer and the worker each possess valuable assets that the other needs. It is therefore wrong to believe that as a job candidate you are at the mercy of the person interviewing you.

One of you is buying, and one of you is selling. Both of you have power in the interview and over its outcome. A successful relationship can be established in an interview if power and control are respected and balanced. What we are going to discuss is *when* you should exert your control and how to benefit from understanding the back-and-forth flow of control.

Jack can help us see how a relationship evolves during an interview. The successful formation of this relationship will make you stand apart from all other candidates for the job. It will prevent your meeting from turning into a dull, unproductive question-and-answer interview.

When Jack meets with a prospective client, his *goal* is to land a suitable consulting contract. His *strategy* in the meeting is to show that he can solve the client's problem. He has to execute his strategy before he can achieve his goal.

A good consultant's strategy is based on the Four Questions. By working through each of them, a consultant like Jack can give his prospective client compelling reasons for hiring him. The strategy has worked if the client agrees that Jack can do the job. Jack then takes up his goal and negotiates a deal that is suitable to him. This usually includes not only a fee, but the exact project description (which is also negotiable), the resources he will be given to do it, the scope of his authority, the extent of his responsibility, and so on.

Job candidates should think of themselves as consultants when they go into an interview. Each must understand the "client's" needs and prove he can satisfy them. Then he can get his own terms and needs met, once the client decides this is the person to hire for the job.

Too often, job candidates confuse the *locus* (or source) *of control* in an interview, because it shifts during a successful meeting. As host of the meeting, the employer is in control to start. He is footing the bill. It is his need that gave rise to the meeting. This is why *doing the job*, or satisfying his need, is paramount in the interview. Almost paradoxically, this is also the mechanism that causes control to shift to the successful candidate. The employer needs the candidate to get a job done, just as he depends on a consultant to take responsibility to do the work.

When the client first meets with a consultant, he fully expects and hopes the consultant will prove he can do the job. It is no different for a job candidate. As Jack would say, "What else are you there for, if not to do the job!" That is why I say an employer wants nothing more than to hire you. You are there to do the job, and the "client" hopes he won't have to bother talking to more candidates.

> The smart candidate respects the locus of control when the interview begins, but he also knows that he has to tip the scales to bring the control toward himself. He respects the employer's needs and addresses them *before bringing up his own*. This is where the leverage lies in an interview. Proceeding through the Four Questions, the candidate gradually demonstrates compelling proof that he can satisfy the employer's needs.

To achieve the shift in control, the candidate must progress through the Four Questions and demonstrate to the employer that he:

- understands what work has to be done;
- can do the work;
- can do it the way the employer wants it done; and
- can do it profitably for the employer.

Once the employer is convinced, and decides he wants to hire the candidate, the locus of control shifts to the candidate. The employer then has to convince the candidate to take the job. The candidate is finally in the right position to negotiate the deal he wants if, in fact, he wants the job.

After a traditional interview, this shift in control can take days or weeks. This is the waiting period during which the employer decides whether to entrust the job to one candidate or another. This is the period every candidate dreads and wants to avoid.

All along, we have been discussing a method to force this shift in control to happen quickly, during the New Interview, while the iron is hot.

Doing the job causes the most rapid shift in control that I know. There is nothing more compelling than doing the job, if you want to get the employer's attention. Few, if any, job candidates attempt it. *Doing the job* will put you in a class by yourself.

Do the Job During the Interview

Hitting on All Cylinders

Gerry Zagorski got his dream job while he was still going to college: working for a well-known computer company for great pay. Gerry was no slouch. Before long, he had worked his way into sales. He won commendations and awards on assignment after assignment. When the company downsized, Gerry was retained. In fact, he was promoted. By the time I met him, he was the top sales manager in his region. When he hit his seventeenth year with the company, I got a call.

"Nick, you know how loyal I've been to this company. They've been good to me. I've built my life here. Now here's what's been bothering me. I could plug along and be safe and retire on this job—but I'd go crazy. The other choice is to go for the brass ring. I want more challenges; I don't want to be an on-the-job retiree. I've decided it's time for a change. So, I'm going to interview with a communications company in a couple of weeks."

Gerry's loyalty to his company was legendary, but I wasn't surprised. "I understand," I said. "I've been watching you grow increasingly restless and bored!"

"There's one problem. I haven't interviewed for a job in seventeen years, except here internally. I really need your help. What do I do?" Gerry asked anxiously. The opportunity he described was outstanding. Other jobs might come along, but this one was a peach. If he wasn't going to take this job, he wanted it to be *his* decision, not because he didn't get an offer.

I sent Gerry a copy of my guide. He read it and called me. "Looks like I've got some homework to do, huh?"

"Call me when you get done with the interview," I replied. His next call came about a week later.

"Well?" I asked, eager to know how this talented salesman had fared on his very first job hunting venture.

"I did exactly what you suggested. I still can't believe it—the message in the book was to do in the interview what I do every day: the work I'm good at. I walked in, shook the vice president's hand, and exchanged pleasantries. He asked if it was okay if he ate his lunch during our meeting. That was kind of odd, but I agreed. Then he told me our interview would only be twenty minutes long.

"Twenty minutes! But that was exactly what I had prepared for— a hard-core demonstration of what I do best. I said, 'I don't really want to waste this time on where I went to school and what my last three titles were. Let me tell you what I know about *your* business and the challenges you're facing, and then I'll *show* you how I'm going to help make your business more profitable. Can I use your whiteboard?' "

"And what happened?" I prodded him.

"Well," Gerry chuckled, "the manager got this real big smile on his face and he waved me over to the board. 'Go for it,' he said. I could just see the look in his eyes: 'Let's just give this guy all the rope he wants . . .' "

Gerry did fifteen minutes of his planned presentation. As he drew a line across the bottom of the whiteboard and wrote down his estimate of what he thought he could bring to the bottom line, he looked up at his interviewer.

"The guy's jaw was on the floor. Not because of the number I put down—turns out I was way off. But he stopped me right there and told me to sit down. 'You don't need to do any more,' he said. 'And I don't need to interview you. I've been waiting for somebody like you to walk in here for months. Mind if some of the other members of my team come in? We've got work to do.'

"Nick, it was zero to sixty in nothing flat! Every cylinder was cranking and I knew I was doing the driving! The meeting lasted almost two hours and there was no standard interview nonsense. My demonstration changed the whole tone. I met everyone on the team and it felt like I was at work already. And the guy never finished his sandwich!"

The computer company made a healthy counteroffer, and Gerry agonized about making the change—he had a lot invested in his old job. He wanted a new challenge, but he also wanted an offer that wouldn't make him think twice about leaving his seniority and years of accumulated benefits behind. Convinced he had done all his homework on this new company and that he had demonstrated hands-down how he could help them improve profits, Gerry stood on his value and negotiated further. After one more meeting, the communications company made him an outstanding second offer.

Gerry has never looked back. Today, he is managing business development for this company's most important sales region, and his new employer has more than earned back the investment they made in hiring Gerry.

Doing the job during the interview is the most powerful way to control an interview. However, it requires a lot of preparation—so much preparation that you will decline interviews if they are not worth the effort. Gerry went after a job he really wanted and he did a lot of work to win it. But that's how it should be. If a job is worth wanting, it's worth preparing for.

You have selected a worthwhile job. Let's look at how you can tackle it. How do you "do the job" before you have the job?

> You do the job during the interview by solving some of the problems that led the employer to create the job in the first place.

The preparation* you have done will help you identify and understand the problems the company is facing. Gerry didn't spend the two weeks before his interview mailing out résumés to other companies. He spent it identifying problems that he could solve during the interview itself.

Your challenge is to do the necessary research and to encourage the employer to talk with you about his problems, so that you can present solutions. You will jump-start this new job by creating an opportunity to do the job in the interview.

Let's take a look at two ways that you can *do the job* in your meeting. Both methods require that you have a solid understanding of both the company and the industry it is in. Both approaches might seem a little scary. It takes a confident person to take the risk of controlling the interview. It's risky because if you're not prepared, you'll blow it. If you are prepared, your confidence will pave the way for success with either approach.

Much of this book is directed at helping you understand how to enter an interview powerfully and confidently—you can't just try to "do the job" without studying the rest of this book. If you have done your preparation, if you are truly good at your work, and if you have selected the right job opportunity, everything we talk about next will come to you comfortably.

> WARNING: The two methods of doing the job in the interview that follow are intended to be used when you interview with the *hiring manager*. They are not intended for use with a personnel representative or any other go-between.

*This preparation is covered in detail in chapter 5.

Interactive Method

Through your interaction with the hiring manager during the interview, you decide what problem you are going to solve for him. You do it "on the fly" because you were not able to get a lot of information from him prior to your meeting. Use the interactive method to take complete control of an interview when the employer isn't giving you enough room to demonstrate your abilities.

In the example that follows, you are a salesperson interviewing for a job at a computer company. Underlined text indicates the important points that can be generalized to apply to almost any job and any problem an employer is facing. Follow these points to help an employer solve a real problem.

1. First, you must decide what problem you are going to solve or what job you are going to do, for the manager. The best way to do this is to ask, point-blank, <u>what problem the manager hopes to solve by hiring you, or how you can help make his business more profitable.</u> The problem may be as general as "I need to increase sales," or it may be more specific. It may take a little discussion to identify what the manager really needs; he's not accustomed to people making such an offer.

    Let's say that during the meeting you learn that the employer's problem is the inability to break into a new group of accounts in the pharmaceutical industry. <u>The employer should describe this problem in his own words.</u> Usually, all it takes is asking some simple questions relating to challenges and desired accomplishments: <u>What's your toughest challenge (or problem) in your market today? What above all else would you like a new employee to accomplish?</u>

2. You already have some idea about the challenges a computer company is facing, because you have read up on the

current state of the industry. Your challenge is to use everything you know to solve the specific problem the manager has posed. You don't have to be very detailed, and your solution doesn't have to be the best one. It just needs to be a good, thoughtful one. <u>Your goal is to show the manager how you think and how you work. Most important, you want him to see your enthusiasm and your commitment to your work. Tell the manager, "Let me show you in a little detail how I would tackle this problem. Is it okay if I draw some things out on paper [or on a whiteboard]?"</u>

3. Make sure you understand the problem clearly. <u>Write the problem down.</u> Ask for more detail if you need it. Does the manager agree that this is the problem? If not, restate it together.

   Make sure you also understand what goal the manager is working toward: higher sales? more profit? penetration of an account at any cost? <u>Write down the goal.</u> Your task is to show how it can be achieved. Make sure the manager can see what you're writing.

4. <u>Use graphics.</u> <u>Sketch the problem out diagrammatically, listing the factors that affect the company's ability to solve it.</u> List the <u>obstacles</u> the computer company faces (ask the employer to add to the list). Review the <u>resources</u> the company can use to overcome these obstacles.

   <u>Draw boxes and arrows, indicating the relationships among the problem, the goal, and the resources that will be available to you. Include a list of special skills that you will bring to the company.</u>

5. List what you believe to be the <u>needs</u> of the particular customer (the pharmaceutical company, in this example). <u>Highlight the measures you would take to solve the problem and reach the goal using the resources and your skills. If you need special tools, draw them in, too.</u>

Encourage the manager to comment during this task. Ask him to add details where he sees fit. <u>Get the manager's input</u> on your analysis.

6. <u>Summon up everything you have learned about this company's business and every ounce of your knowledge and skill</u> about selling computers into new accounts. <u>Present a simple strategy</u> that will get you in the door to meet with important people in these "problem" accounts.

   <u>List the specific things you would do.</u> For example, cold-call fifty people at each account, meet with key department heads, solicit leads from other pharmaceutical companies, and so on. <u>Use ideas that worked for you on similar challenges in the past. Use ideas for which you have been rewarded.</u> Encourage the manager to comment and add his ideas.

   Notice that you're not talking about your experience or recounting marvelous stories about past successes here—you are showing the manager how you are going to actually do the job he needs to have done.

   <u>Explain exactly what you would do tomorrow if you were on the job</u> to put your strategy and tactics to work immediately. Remember to <u>tackle the issue of profitability: how is your way of doing this work going to help reduce costs and/or increase revenues? Put a number on it. The number may not be right, but you should be ready to defend it intelligently.</u>

7. Now <u>show how you would use other resources in the company, including people and processes.</u> For example, how can the service manager help crack these accounts? Does he have any special programs in place that you could leverage to win the account? How can the marketing department participate? Are they running any special promotions? <u>How could the interviewer's own skills be applied to the project?</u> What's his greatest skill? How could you put him to best use in a sales presentation?

Suggest that other relevant managers and staff members participate in your discussion. In this example, that might include the service manager and the marketing manager. Your particular situation might require the participation of other team members or support staff. Offer to come back for a live meeting with them, with a more specific plan of attack. Your goal here is to show that you work well with others.

8. The key is to show your grasp of the problem, and to convince the manager that it matters to you. Act like you are on the job, and like the interviewer is your boss. He expects you to do your job and solve this problem. You will earn a handsome bonus (a new job) if you succeed. Let your excitement build up, and let it out! Solve the problem the best way you know how!

9. Finally, ask him to grade you. Tell him you want to know what he thinks are the strengths and weaknesses of your approach. What would he want you to change in your approach? Does he agree that your strategy will work? What does he think of your profit estimate?

Presentation Method

If you can obtain enough of the right information prior to your interview, you can prepare a structured presentation. This method involves as much background research as the interactive method, but it requires extra preparation because you must define a problem the manager needs solved *before you go into the interview.*

You may have learned about such a problem by talking to the manager on the phone, or by talking with other employees of the company. Good industry publications are rife with articles about issues that are currently critical. Preferably, the problem should be one faced by the industry as a whole—one that can be adequately analyzed by you without requiring too much specific information. If the problem is too specific, you will run the unnecessary risk of misinterpreting it.

In any case, you need to get the manager's cooperation to do this. Don't go into the interview planning to do a presentation without getting his approval beforehand. Here are a couple of ways to get his cooperation on the phone before your meeting.

I'd like to make this interview a little different for you. I'm not out interviewing because I need to "get a job." I'm looking for the right job, where I can do what I'm expert at, in a way that will be profitable for your company. If you'll let me take a few minutes at the beginning of our meeting, I would like to demonstrate to you how I would do this job. I think that will make it easier for you to decide if I'm the person you want to hire, and for me to decide if this is the right job for me.

Or, you might take this approach:

May I make your task of evaluating me easier? Let me show you how much I know about your business, and how I think I can help you. I don't just want to talk theoretically, I want to show you. I want to demonstrate to you how I would do this job. I know I'm taking a risk, but if I can't prove to you that I can do this job, there is no reason for you to hire me. Will you give me a few minutes in our meeting to do this?

If he agrees, you're in a good position to prepare a presentation. You just need to decide on which problem or challenge you will focus. Remember that you will have already done some research, and you should have a good idea about what kind of work the manager's team is tackling. Let him know you've done your homework, and that you want him to confirm that you're on the right track. Here's how to find out, while you're still on the phone with the manager.

From what I understand about your team, you're looking for someone to [describe the work as you understand it]. I want to make sure I know what's important to you before we meet. How would you characterize the main problem, or challenge, you want a new employee to handle? In our meeting, I'll show you how I would tackle it.

This approach should get you the information you will need to build your presentation. If you need more details than the manager gave you, ask him more questions about it. A good manager will recognize a motivated job candidate and he'll talk with you. (Don't get discouraged if the manager won't cooperate. Instead, think about whether you would really want to work for him.) If you need to, rely on your research to help you define the challenge more clearly (see "The Power of Information," in chapter 6).

Remember, you're going to do a presentation. Therefore, you are responsible for directing it. Make sure the manager understands this. He's probably so accustomed to the standard Q&A interview format that he might forget what's going on. Remind him. Explain that your presentation will take about twenty minutes, so that he can ask questions and discuss other issues during the rest of the meeting.

You will use the Four Questions to guide you. Keep each of the four parts of the presentation brief and to the point. The manager can get into more detail after your presentation is complete. In the following example, underlined text indicates the key points.

1. *Prove that you understand the job that needs to be done.*

   Start by describing the problem or challenge the manager seems to be facing. Have him confirm it. Write it down. Restate the problem as a goal, to make clear what you're trying to achieve in your demonstration. Again, have the manager confirm it. Write the goal down so the manager can see it. Make sure the problem and the goal correspond. Describe the job that needs to be done, as you understand it. <u>Describe two or three examples of tasks that are involved in doing the job.</u> Ask the manager if he would like to supply better examples. <u>Create simple diagrams or sketches while you are talking.</u> If possible, do these on a whiteboard, or on a piece of paper on the manager's desk. If you can manage it, sit to the side of the manager's desk rather than in front of it, so both of you can read the diagrams. <u>Welcome the manager to make corrections and comments.</u> Spend about five minutes on this part.

2. *Show that you can do the job.*

Use the diagrams to <u>show what strategies you would use and what steps you would follow to perform the tasks, solve the problem, and achieve the goal</u> you wrote down earlier. <u>Talk about the tools you would use</u> (conceptual tools like market studies, physical tools like computers, or other people on the team). <u>List these tools beside your diagrams.</u> Refer to the interactive method (page 84) for more ideas about how to lay out this part of your presentation. Five minutes is not a lot of time to do this part, but you should try to limit it to that amount.

3. *Show that you can do the job the way the manager wants it done.*

Ask the manager <u>what is most important to him about how to do the job right.</u> Now "redo" the tasks if necessary, taking the manager's requirements into account. <u>Ask the manager to confirm his satisfaction with your approach.</u> If he's not satisfied, find out why and explain how you would reshape your approach. If you're going to go beyond five minutes on a section, this is the one. <u>The manager's approval of your approach is critical. If you don't get it right here, you will not get it right on the job.</u>

4. *Show that you can do the job profitably for the company.*

<u>Explain how your work would affect the company's profitability.</u> <u>Show on your diagrams where and how</u>

profitability could be improved, and how you would improve it. Ask the manager to make his own suggestions. Your twenty minutes are up.

When you're finished, ask the manager to grade you, as in the interactive method (see page 86).

Obviously, this presentation may take longer than twenty minutes, especially if the manager gets involved. Go with the flow. If he follows your lead and uses your presentation as the heart of the interview, you have succeeded in controlling the interview and in taking him with you. No other candidate will be able to touch you.

Tackling a Live Problem

By using the interactive or presentation method, you set the stage to enable the manager to evaluate you in a way far more powerful than any offered by a traditional interview. Don't be surprised if he wants to spend more time with you, exploring your capabilities and his problems. Gerry Zagorski brought his interview to this level, and before the manager knew what was happening, the two had rolled up their sleeves for a hands-on working meeting. Once the work started, the traditional interrogation was left behind.

Whether the interviewer continues on the stage you have set or switches back to a question-and-answer format, you can take the *do the job* approach another step forward later in the interview. At a comfortable point, ask the manager to "put the toughest problem you're dealing with on the table. Let's deal with a live one. I'd like to show you how I can help you solve it. We probably won't solve it right here and now, but both of us will learn how well we can work together."

This is more than a demonstration. You will be working with the manager on a live project as a member of his team. Invite the manager to draw some pictures and state the goal. Create more drawings, lists, or diagrams to help simplify the definition of the problem. <u>Act like the project manager on this task. Take the lead. Don't wait for him to do the work while you watch. Give the manager the opportunity to view you as a valuable employee rather than a job candidate. Act like a consultant. Act like you have the job, and the company's success depends on your doing it right.</u> Together, create a strategy to tackle the problem, and go over the tasks that need to be accomplished to solve it.

During this work session, refer to profitability issues. <u>How will each idea discussed affect the profitability of the company?</u> Are there more cost-effective ways to do the job? Will an idea cost less now, but ultimately cost more later?

In the midst of this process, ask if there are <u>other members of the manager's team</u> that he might want to have participate in the meeting. Tell him you would like to at least meet them. <u>Ask to see the tools</u> his department uses on this kind of project. <u>Ask to tour the facility</u> to see where and how the work actually gets done. <u>Ask to meet the people who support the job</u> you would be doing. If there's no time to do this, <u>suggest a follow-up visit</u> to meet these people. Explain that it is important to you to know how you will fit in with the people you would be working with if you take the job.

Each of these requests reflects your attention to the details of doing the job. A good employer will immediately recognize that your concern is with the work itself, not with getting a job.

We have covered a lot of ideas about what you can say and do to communicate your ability to do a job. Because the requirements of jobs vary, and each interview is different, you must use your judgment about which ideas to use and how to apply them. Be careful not to overdo it. Don't overwhelm the interviewer, or overtax yourself.

For each opportunity you pursue, ask and answer the Four Questions and review the interactive and presentation methods for doing the job in the interview. Consider how you would apply these methods to the specific opportunity. Refer to the summary "Keys to Doing the Job in the Interview" on page 93. Use this summary to outline a presentation to win a job in which you think you are interested.

Back to Control

An employer will quite naturally share control with you in an interview when he sees that your goal is not to "get" the job, but to *do the job*. He has already met with too many candidates whose first interest is a paycheck.

> The tone of the interview will change; you will be able to feel it. Both you and the manager will become aware that you are working with him *like a member of his team* to solve his problems and get a job done, rather than being interviewed.

The distinction between *getting* and *doing* is critical. It is the difference between taking and giving. When you give something of true value, like your expertise, you make yourself bigger. You add to your worth and make yourself more desirable.

The concept of taking control in an interview should be very clear to you now. By focusing on *doing the job*, you take responsibility for—and control over—an interview. By giving an employer *compelling proof* that you can do the job, *you solve his problem* and the power in the relationship tips in your direction. Now he needs you.

If the employer indicates that he'd like you to join his team, tell him you'd like nothing better than to have a specific offer to consider. But don't accept his offer on the spot. When you go on an interview, you always take the risk of being rejected. When an employer makes an offer, he takes the same risk. Take your time; the employer did. It's okay to make a commitment to the job by saying you want it, but don't make a commitment to the offer until you've had time to consider it, and possibly to negotiate it. We'll be discussing how to handle the offer stage of the interview in The Power of the Offer section of chapter 6.

Keys to Doing the Job in the Interview

Preliminary research — Gather all necessary information about the company, manager, and job prior to the interview.

Manager defines the problem — Get the manager to state the problem in his words. Write it down. State it in your own words. Have him confirm your understanding.

Manager defines his goal — Get the manager to state the goal in his words. The goal must be related to the problem. Write it down. Have him confirm it.

Show your enthusiasm — Be focused, be serious, and be enthusiastic.

Factor in your industry knowledge — Make sure you understand the problem and goal in light of the state of the industry. Use everything you know. This is not a drill.

Draw a picture — Include the problem, the goal, and the resources available (these will include people, especially others employed by the company).

Draw relationships — Use lines and arrows to show how the resources will be applied to solve the problem and achieve the goal. Indicate factors that will affect the quality, cost, and profitability of the solution. Show what obstacles will appear, how you would overcome them, and how long it will take. Note any special tools or resources you will need and show how they will be used.

Show your special skills — Fill in and describe the special skills you possess that will enable you to achieve the goal, including skills using special tools.

Define a simple strategy — At the bottom of your drawings, briefly write out a simple strategy you will use to achieve the goal. Show how you will do the job!

Describe the specific tasks	List the specific things you would do to implement your strategy if you were on the job today. The list should be in the form of steps that anyone at the company would understand. Use proven ideas that you believe in. Highlight your special abilities.
Apply company resources	Demonstrate your knowledge of the company's resources, including people and departments. How would you utilize them?
Apply the manager's skills	Show how you would make best use of the interviewer's (your future boss's) skills and abilities. Get him involved.
Get the manager's input	Are you doing the work the way the manager wants it done? Ask him for comments, suggestions, and guidance. Ask where in this project he would want to be involved, and how.
Review profitability	Explain why you think your approach will be profitable to the company. Ask the manager if he agrees. Find out what "profitability" means to him as far as this job is concerned.
Close the loop	Restate the goal, summarize your approach and the reasons it will work, and explain how the company will profit from it.
Ask for a grade	Ask the manager to give you a grade for your work. Ask him to comment on the strengths/weaknesses of your approach. What changes would he make? Does he agree your strategy will work?

Don't Suck Canal Water
Trying to Swallow a Broken Job

Every now and then, you will run into a really difficult interview situation. Even after you've done all your research and prepared yourself in every conceivable way, you will encounter a manager who is conducting interviews to fill a job that doesn't work. The job is broken. There are many such jobs. If you apply the Four Questions both before and during an interview, you will avoid getting hired to fail at one. You will also avoid wasting your time sucking canal water. That's what happens in an interview when you suddenly get a bad taste in your mouth because you suspect the manager doesn't know what he's talking about. If you let the interview continue on such a track, you will be gasping for air, and you will be inhaling garbage.

Ed Moreland* applied the Four Questions in just such a situation—and saved himself from a broken job. Ed was a highly qualified candidate interviewing for the position of manager of research operations for a major pharmaceutical company. At the time, Ed held a similar position with a competing firm. He interviewed with the executive to whom the position would report.

Ed was conquering every aspect of the interview, and it seemed the executive was on the brink of deciding to hire him. In spite of the reinforcing feedback Ed was getting, something was bothering him. He sensed that something wasn't right at a critical level of detail. When the man who would be his boss asked Ed if he had any other questions, Ed leaned forward in his chair.

"I want to make sure we understand the job the same way. It might help if we work through an example together. Could you lay out a live problem for me—without divulging any proprietary or confidential information, of course—a problem that you're facing right now and that you would want me to tackle if you hired me?"

The executive sat back in his chair. Clearly the interview had just shifted gears. Ed was struck by the profound silence as the manager

*Not his real name.

across from him sat thinking. The silence wasn't uncomfortable, but a few minutes went by. It was easy to see that this man was considering Ed's question very seriously. Finally he looked up at Ed.

"I really can't think of one," he admitted, seeming surprised at himself. "I just can't think of one."

The meeting ended amiably. Nonetheless, Ed left the executive's office feeling disconcerted and confused. "We discussed the company's mission, the philosophy of the research department, and we even talked about some of the work the last guy in the job had done."

A week later, Ed called his contact at the company—the person who had introduced him and gotten him the interview—to ask if she'd heard anything about the job.

"Oh. You don't know? They decided not to fill the job after all," she replied. "Don't feel bad. From what I heard, it didn't have anything to do with you. They just decided the position was unnecessary."

Ed called me shortly afterwards to say that now he understood exactly what I meant by a broken job. "I don't know for sure, but I think I helped the manager realize there really wasn't any specific work that needed doing."

What went wrong? Sometimes a manager is in such a hurry to fill out his head count that he doesn't stop to consider whether any specific work needs to be done. Or, a desperate manager tries to throw more bodies at a problem he doesn't really understand himself. For whatever reason, he ends up creating broken jobs *because he is not really thinking about the work*. Henry Thoreau once said, "It is a characteristic of wisdom not to do desperate things." It takes a desperate manager to create a broken job, and that's not smart.

A job is broken when no clear goals have been established for it. No one seems to know exactly what tasks the worker is supposed to accomplish. The work is usually so disorganized that it's impossible for the manager to measure your performance. Anyone who tries to do this type of job will fail. But it doesn't stop some managers from filling the job anyway. In Ed's case, the employer came face-to-face with his folly during the interview.

Interviewing for a broken job can be daunting for the candidate, because the manager can't really describe the work. Oh, he can outline the "position." He can say what a "challenge" it is. But he will avoid actually talking much about the specific work. And, unless someone asks the Four Questions, neither the employer nor the candidate will realize that the job is not doable. You see, the Four Questions cut two ways: the employer must have answers for them, too. If an employer cannot describe the work in detail, or is not interested in seeing how you would do it, you must make a choice. Do you want to work for such a manager?

Use the Four Questions to weed out broken jobs either before or during the interview. If the employer can't or won't describe the job in enough detail so that you can demonstrate how you would do it, and if he can't tell you how your performance will be measured, run, don't walk, to the exit.

How do you know whether a job is broken? Your gut will probably tell you that something is wrong. If the interview gets confusing and you know you're not causing the confusion, go with your gut. Ask for *the manager's version* of a written description of the job, as well as written goals and milestones that are to be achieved. Most important, find out how your performance will be measured and on what basis you will be reviewed for promotion. You will quickly discover whether the manager has really thought this out.

There is one another option, if you have the stomach for it. If you have established a strong enough rapport with the employer, you can come right out and tell him that you think the job is broken. You can offer to collaborate with him to figure out what work really needs to be done, so that a legitimate job can be created. If he agrees, you may find yourself in the enviable position of designing your own job. It could also be a waste of your time. Use your judgment. The Four Questions will help you identify broken jobs so you can decide how to deal with them.

CHAPTER 5

Master Your Attitude

Be an Employee, Not a Candidate

An employer has very little time to get to know you in an interview. He will learn a little about your work skills, but he will learn a lot about your attitude. People tend to judge a book by its cover, and they tend to judge one another on first impressions. Your attitude, more than anything else, affects the impression others form about you. In an interview, the attitude you project is absolutely critical, and you will reap incredible rewards by mastering it.

Throughout this book, we have talked about how the employment industry has placed the job hunter in a subservient position in the hiring process. It's no wonder people have poor attitudes about job hunting and interviewing. They feel degraded by this impersonal system that seems incapable of recognizing who they really are. The best way to develop a good attitude is to *open your mind* and *see yourself in a new light.*

My goal is to show you that you are a powerful force and that you can exert great control in an interview. You don't need to pretend, or to "psych yourself up," to do well in an interview. You just need to see yourself for what you really are: the solution to a manager's problem.

People get nervous about interviews because they feel they're walking into a situation they don't control. They don't like to ask someone for a job. Being in this "asking" role can be very intimidating. This perceived lack of control can also be debilitating when, in an interview, you're trying to focus on performing at your best.

You're in a strange office, meeting someone you don't know who can offer you a job—someone who is considering lots of other candidates for the same job. No matter how good you are at your work, this person potentially holds the keys to your future. He owns the job you want. And he may not even like you! Boy, does that make him godlike! You feel like a kid in the principal's office.

But wait a minute! What are we talking about? You came to the interview prepared and confident about your skills and ability to do the job. There's no weakness. If you're really prepared, all you need to do is master *your attitude about interviewing* by locking onto the following approach:

1. Everything you know about interviewing is wrong. An interview is not an interrogation. You are not a horse waiting to have its teeth examined before it's sold. You are here to grant the manager's wish to solve his problems.

2. Make sure you possess all the knowledge you possibly can about all aspects of the job, about the company, and about the manager. This will give you confidence and the tools you need to succeed. Most important, it will make you as powerful as the hiring manager in the interview.

3. Act as if you're the solution to the manager's problem: this is how he wants to perceive you. Imagine that you are a consultant who is ready to get down to work *in the interview*. Act like you're already on the payroll.

4. Finally, you must be ready to do the job well. You must be of one mind with the work and help the manager see not only

your abilities, but also the *outcome* of applying your abilities to the work. Prove that you will be a profitable addition to his team.

> If you go into an interview intending only to answer an interviewer's questions, you give the interviewer total control. *If you go into an interview to do the work you are expert at, you assume control.* This control will give you a powerful attitude.

A consultant would never go through the office door without having done all his homework. A consultant knows a lot about his client's problem in advance, and he has many of the right answers in his pocket. Why else would the manager hire him? Why else would he hire *you?* You have to be at least as good as a consultant.

Your attitude must be centered not on the traditional structure of the interview but on the needs of the employer: "I'm here to take care of your problem." If you approach your meeting this way, the employer will be at your feet.

You must be *at work and on the job* in the interview. You are not there to sit quietly and answer questions. You are there to work with the manager to solve his problems. You are there to *do the job.*

> Don't be a candidate, be an employee. This attitude produces a job offer.

Honesty Is Power

Your effectiveness in interviews depends in large part on how honest you are with yourself about the particular job for which you are interviewing. If you are honest with yourself, you will relax in an interview and talk about the things that matter. You will hear the interviewer better, and you will have a professional dialogue. If you're not honest with yourself, don't read any further. You're wasting your time. Stop here, take a look at yourself in the mirror, and have a talk with yourself about who you are, what your skills are, what you want, and what value you have to offer. You will know whether you are being honest with yourself by asking and answering the Four Questions about a particular job.

The most effective way to succeed in your job search is to pursue the right job. As a headhunter, I have met many professionals who just wanted a job. Not concerned enough with the work itself, they wanted to either get away from the job they already had or get the first job they could find that paid more money.

When a person interviews for a job for one or both of those reasons, he is being dishonest with himself and with the employer. He is dishonest because his intent is at odds with the intent of the employer. He is not focused on doing the work. This attitude will turn the interview into a battle of wits rather than a meeting of minds.

The Four Questions will help you to develop a new level of honesty about your job goals. Pursue a job because you want to do the work. The honesty of that action will make you a powerful candidate for the job. It will also make you worth more as an employee.

I have met many people who, although they work hard (maybe *because* they work hard), let themselves slide on the issue of being honest about the career choices they make. I want to especially encourage these people to think carefully about every job opportunity they encounter.

Sometimes a person is not even actively looking for a job. A job comes along and sort of bites him in the pants. He thinks he wants it just because someone tells him it is available. Or because being offered a new job makes him feel desirable.

People like this tend to be *reactive*. They do not make decisions; instead, they react to circumstances. If they don't like their boss or feel unappreciated, they're ripe for a change. Eager for something different, they usually take the first thing that comes along. More often than not, they jump out of the frying pan into the fire.

Their new situation offers no better prospects than they had in their last job.

So, ask yourself the Four Questions not only about the job you are considering but about your present job. Are you focused on your work? If not, you're not likely to focus on the work in an interview for another job.

I met one highly educated, skilled engineer who held four jobs with four different companies in one year. It was not because he got fired or laid off. He pursued each of these jobs with a purpose—to get a bigger paycheck. As soon as he landed one job, he would approach another company, show them how much he was making, and ask for an additional 10 percent. Because his skills were in demand, he would get hired each time for a little more money. At one point, he was actually working for two companies at the same time without either knowing it. His career plan was to make as much money as he could. The job and the company did not matter, as long as an employer could meet his price.

In just a year, he realized a sizable salary increase due to the job changes. Yet his satisfaction with his work was low. His involvement was minimal. He did whatever he had to do just to get by.

Because his skills were in great demand, I could have placed him quickly into yet another job and earned a large fee. But he lacked the one thing I based my reputation on: honesty. I could not in good faith recommend him to any of my clients because he would never give them an honest day's work. His real work was interviewing and finding new jobs. But employers don't knowingly pay for that kind of work.

> If you spend most of your time thinking about finding your next job, how much of your time are you spending making your current job the right job?

You may find that you do not need a new job if you give your current job an honest chance. Make sure you are doing an honest day's work. A person who produces high-quality work is worth what he's being paid. When he seeks a new job, he is also worth what he's asking.

If you are unhappy with your current employment, make sure you know what you're worth and what makes you valuable to your company. Are you using your skills to help make your company more profitable? Apply the Four Questions to your job. If you think you can do more and should be paid more for it, then interview with your own company for a raise or a better position.

When you interview for a new job, an employer will sense your dedication to your work—or the lack of it. Attitude always shows. This will tell him all he needs to know about how honest you are. If you don't give your all to your present job, what will you give to a new one?

Jobs aren't about money, success, or recognition. They are about the work you do. If you do good work, the money, success, and recognition follow.

WORKSHEET 7:
ARE YOU ACTIVE IN YOUR PROFESSIONAL COMMUNITY?

If you are an active member of your professional community, you are always on the path to your next good job, whether it is within your current company or in a new one. Workers who stay abreast of current industry issues, participate in industry education, and contribute to the health and growth of their industry are, by definition, desirable workers. This exercise will help gauge whether you are in position for professional growth. You should create a separate table of answers for each item below.

1. Think about people in your industry that you've talked with in the past year about your industry. (These should not include people in your company, people you have ever been employed by, or people who have interviewed you for a job.)

   A. Which *acknowledged experts* in your industry have you talked with (a) on the phone, and (b) face to face? List names and affiliations.

   B. What *other* industry people have you talked with (a) on the phone, and (b) face to face? List names. (Think of people in other companies you have "partnered" with on a project, or with whom you have competed.)

2. What industry seminars, conventions, or meetings did you attend in the last twelve months where the participants came from more than one company? Who were the speakers at these meetings? The chairpersons?

3. What courses have you taken in the last twelve months that are relevant to your industry or business? Who were the instructors? What companies do they work for? Who were the students in your classes? What companies do they work for?

4. Think about the last time you were asked for your professional advice or guidance by someone who does the same kind of work you do but who does not work for your company. Has anyone ever asked you for such help? Were you able to give it? Did your help make a difference? How?

The number of people you have been in contact with will vary depending on your business and your industry. You should be able to judge for yourself whether you have any real involvement with your industry beyond your own employer.

If the numbers look small to you, make a special effort to meet and talk with experts in your industry, to participate in industry events and continuing education, and to make an active contribution to the state of the art in your industry. These contacts and experiences are the true resources that make you a valuable worker. These are also the people who will help you find your next job.

Don't Compete with Yourself

It is said that a person can be his own worst enemy. In other words, a person can undermine his own efforts without realizing it. This is a common occurrence in an interview: you try to perform well, but you inadvertently do things that prevent you from achieving your goal. How does this happen?

Sometimes, you know what you want, but you have not done what is necessary to achieve it. You are *unprepared*. Perhaps you didn't know where to get the information you needed to prepare for your meeting. Perhaps you just didn't devote enough time to studying and thinking. Or, you thought you knew everything, but you were wrong. Whatever the reason, you have sabotaged your own efforts. The ignorant part of you is competing with the part of you that wants the job. Which part do you think will win?

You also undermine your efforts when you are *not in control of yourself*—when you're scared, nervous, apprehensive, or lack confidence. Some of the most talented, prepared people fall apart when they have to "perform" in an interview. If they can't perform, it doesn't matter how skilled they are. The capable part of them is competing with the scared part. The stronger part will win.

Preparedness

You can sit in an interview and talk all you want about yourself, your experience, your accomplishments, your skills, your strengths, and your past jobs. But you will be sabotaging yourself if you don't talk about the one thing that a manager wants to hear about before hiring you: the job. Your interview will be just like all the other misguided interviews that happen every day.

If you're not prepared, you won't be talking about the job because you won't know anything about it, or about the company that owns it, or about the customers who benefit from it. All you can do is fake it. And that's not what this book is about.

There is only one way to prepare yourself: completely. If you are interviewing and you realize you are not prepared, for whatever reason, there is only one solution: be forthright about it. End the interview and tell the manager you are not prepared for what needs to be discussed. Apologize. Ask to reschedule your meeting, if you think you can prepare yourself for it. You will probably not get a second chance, but you can try. Either way, you will leave the interview with a little self-respect.

If you fake it, you might succeed and get an offer. Some interviewers will think you're a pretty good interviewee. But you will have competed with the lowest part of yourself, and your lowest part will have won. Good luck to you and to the guy who hires you.

Defeating Fear

Being completely prepared will go a long way toward reducing your fear. But if this is your first interview after reading this book, you may still feel anxious. Don't be too hard on yourself. It's natural for those old feelings of insecurity to follow you around until you have a couple of new, positive experiences to replace them. Breaking the habit of being fearful takes a little practice. Your old scared self has not yet seen what your new prepared self is capable of achieving.

If you are completely prepared, your fear probably stems from a sense that someone other than you is in control. Someone else is judging you. Doubts creep into your mind. Do I look nervous? Will I say the wrong thing? What if I forget what I know? What if I just clam up and can't talk? What if someone better than me interviews for this job?

You can solve this problem if you understand how fear works. The scared part of you is weak. All it can do is stop you from executing your plan. We all fear the possibility that we will *fail to do what we prepared for and envisioned.* This possibility can be terrifying, especially if you have planned and rehearsed everything you were going to say in the interview. That makes *everything* vulnerable to failure. What if you screw it all up?

Well, what would happen if you shifted gears and didn't try to do *anything* you planned or rehearsed? You can outwit your scared self with spontaneity.

Ask the interviewer to tell you things that you were not able to unearth in your research about his company, his products, his mission, his problems, or how he conducts interviews. There's nothing to be scared of, because you don't have to talk. You are letting him perform. In the process, you are learning something new, something that can help you with this interview.

> Start your meeting by making the interviewer talk. Most interviewers allow time at the start of an interview for idle chat. They're *trying* to relax you. Take advantage of this. Don't wait for the employer to ask you the first question—the question that will force you to begin the planned presentation you're so nervous about. Get the ball rolling on a topic your scared self can't control. *Talk about something you know absolutely nothing about, and which your scared self can't screw up.*

Here are some sample openings:

- How did the company first get into the business it's in?
- Your company has a well-respected product line (or service). Tell me how it earned its reputation.
- Your company is in a tough business. Tell me what your biggest challenges are today. (You can avoid talking much *and* gather critical information you can use later in your meeting.)
- I'd like to make sure we cover everything that's important to you. Tell me how you like to structure your interviews.

Since you're trying to avoid the stress of the prepared presentation, fix just *one* of these openings in your mind. Ask the question while the two of you are moving toward your seats, before the meeting actually starts. Think of the interviewer as an old friend who just started a new job; you're stopping by to visit.

Most interviewers want to help you relax at the beginning of an interview. The more relaxed you are, the easier it will be for them to evaluate you. Anything you do to help them help you will help you both. A few minutes of easy listening and easy talking will relax you and get you familiar with the interviewer's personality. It will take the edge off the meeting and give you a chance to experience a little success. Your scared self will dwindle away as you and the interviewer build a few positive exchanges, no matter how insignificant they seem (see chapter 8). As the interviewer begins talking, your interest in what he is saying will take over and you will join in the conversation.

> Psychological research has shown that the anxiety of tackling a significant goal (like winning a job offer) can be lessened if we have the benefit of some initial small successes on the path to the larger goal. This foundation of success, no matter how minor it seems, can be critical and it can be empowering. A friendly discussion can start building that foundation of success.

As the interview continues, and you get past your fear, remember that your mission is to *do the job* during the interview. You can silence your scared self by telling the interviewer that *doing the job during the interview* is your goal. Get a live problem he's having out on the table and work with him to solve it. Your mission will be revealed, and the interviewer will be impressed with your self-confidence. Your scared self will have nothing left to feed on.

I said earlier that if you are good at your work, you can be good at interviewing. An interview is a showcase for your most powerful skills. You will be in familiar waters if you focus on demonstrating them. After all, an interview is all about what you are very good at: your work.

Interview for the right job. Learn all you can about the company, the manager, and the work that needs to be done. Have faith in your ability to do the work. Practice demonstrating it. All that's left is to break the ice at the beginning of the interview. Remember that an interview is an invitation to do the job. The employer wants to hire you. If you let him, the employer will help you defeat your scared self and win the interview.

Never Compete with Cows

There is a terrible interview fantasy we all have at some point in our lives. You walk through a door and find you are in a waiting room. The interviewer is in the office beyond, talking with another candidate. In the room with you are several other candidates, waiting. You take a seat and wait, too. You gulp. You think, What if these people are better than I am? What if just *one* of them is better?

Would you feel better if you could get rid of half of these people? How about 80 percent of them? Take another look around. Are these candidates really competitors? An associate of mine says that 80 percent of all people are cows. I'm inclined to agree with him.

If you watch cows in a field, you will notice that they don't move around much. They all look and act pretty much alike. They stand around eating grass. Nothing really motivates them. Huge trucks can whiz by them on the road—just a few feet away and at amazing speeds—and they don't seem to notice. You can throw rocks at them and they don't seem to care. You can push them and they'll move wherever you want them to go. At night you can even tip them over while they're sleeping. They lead boring, uneventful lives because they are boring, unconcerned animals.

Eighty percent of people act like cows. They stand around watching the world go by. Like all the other cows, they spend their lives mindlessly following the rules. And when they don't know what the rules are in a particular situation, they stand around and do nothing. When they move, they move as part of the herd.

Don't worry too much about your competition. Most of them

are cows. They will leave such a poor impression on the interviewer that when he meets you, he will be amazed. The cows have primed him to expect unmotivated candidates who will sit in the interview, waiting to answer questions, waiting to be given a job. If you take the initiative and use the Four Questions to guide your interview, you will stand apart from most of your competition. Or, you can act like a cow yourself.

Most cows sit in interviews and wait to be told what to do. They wait to be addressed, or they say nothing. They are there for one reason—to be milked for information about their past. They dutifully answer each question and then wait for the next one. They think about only the things the interviewer asks them about. When the interview is over, they wait to be herded to the door, after a nice handshake. After the interview, they have no more inkling whether they will win the job than they did before the interview. Worst of all, if they really want the job, they never bother to explicitly say so to the employer. They figure that it's his decision. (Remember Bob, the brilliant engineer who couldn't win a job offer in chapter 1?)

Cows all have résumés in one of the popular formats. They all wear the right kinds of spots. They all study the same interview questions and answers. In fact, they are more concerned about the interview than about the work they do. They memorize the right answers to the big questions:

"I do have a weakness, but I overcame it last week."
"In five years, sir, I see myself in your job."
"I left my last job because I was looking for a better opportunity."

And so on.

If you act like a cow during your interview, you too will be herded to the door without ceremony. The job will go to a better candidate. Rise above cowness. Be the best job candidate. Get down to business and start solving problems, right there in the interview. Know exactly what you're there for and make sure the employer knows it, too. Do the job.

A cow worries about what the next interview question will be, and how he will answer it. Don't be a cow. Instead, ask yourself what this manager needs help with. How can you solve this company's problems? How can your expertise improve this company's bottom line? Don't wait to be asked a question. Offer a solution. That's how to deal with most of your competition: step up and *do the job.*

Do the Job, Not the Interview!

Companies invite people to interviews because they need to get a job done. Not because they're handing out jobs to people who will sit through an interview. American workers who must compete in a wildly shifting world economy should think about this distinction more carefully and more often.

Cows believe two things: companies have jobs, and when people need jobs they go to companies to get them. This attitude is a real flaw in our society. It has developed because more and more Americans are convinced that having a job is a right. Having a job is not a right; it is a consequence of your ability and willingness to perform work that enables an employer to meet his goals profitably.

When a job is regarded as a right, the interview loses its value as a tool for matching the best person with the work. The focus of the job hunt shifts from the work itself to the hiring process. Interviews become a misguided effort to *get someone hired*—to fill out the head count—rather than to *get a job done.* Is it any wonder that the job gets lost in a process which focuses on how you fill out a form, what your résumé looks like, and whether you can deliver programmed answers to irrelevant questions?

Employers are often more concerned about whether a candidate does the interview properly than whether he can do the job. That's why they let personnel jockeys who know nothing about the work conduct interviews. This attitude has given rise to millions of pages about every aspect of job hunting, interviewing, and hiring except *doing the job*. This attitude is the cow attitude, and it follows job hunters around wherever they go.

I recently visited two large chain bookstores. I looked through dozens of books about job hunting. Each of these books had a chapter with a title like "10 Things You Must Do to Get an Offer." Neither the ability to do the job nor the importance of demonstrating that you can do the job made it onto any of these lists.

A look at the advice provided by one of the largest national employment news weeklies was even more disappointing. Repeatedly, the editors referred to the *human resources manager* as the person in a company that a job hunter needs to impress. There was no mention of the hiring manager. The cow attitude is hard to lose.

These publications give you the idea that job hunting is an ordeal quite different from what people do at work every day. In fact, interviewing can be so similar to going to work each day that there is little for a good worker to be apprehensive about. But the "experts" have turned interviewing—which is really about something you are already very good at: your job—into something foreign and mysterious. They have turned it into a game only they can teach you how to play.

Take a look at all the books that teach you how to dress, how to look, how to act, how to talk, and what to say and what to avoid saying in an interview. These are the rules of the game. What these rules don't tell you is how a manufacturing manager can improve his yields, how a sales manager can crack a new account, or how a training manager can create better teaching materials.

Don't you wonder why there are no books about how a software engineer could impress his prospective boss in an interview by suggesting a clever way to get around a flat-memory-model limitation? There should be such a book for every profession, because for each profession the advice would be specialized (most of us wouldn't understand it). An expert in each field would have to write each book. The fact is, engineers, programmers, teachers, salesmen, and secretaries have no interest in writing about interviewing. Interviewing is a small part of their career experience.

In the place of job-specific interviewing advice, a handful of self-proclaimed experts write about how interviews should be conducted. Consequently, there are books that "reveal" how anyone can "respond" to the "standard" interview questions, as though the specific profession or field you are in is irrelevant. They want you to believe that if you just follow the basic rules of interviewing, you'll get hired.

Well, I say bunk. Don't do the interview a personnel jockey expects you to do. Go in and do the job the hiring manager needs you to do. Only *you* can do the job. Only *your work skills* will win you your next job offer. The rules of the traditional interview can make it very difficult for a manager to hire the right worker. But if you can avoid the cow attitude and think for yourself, all is not darkness and despair.

In spite of personnel jockeys, companies still manage to hire the best workers they can find. *Getting a job* might be a game to some people, but *doing a job* is not a game to a good manager. He needs the right worker, not a cow. He will plow through countless wrong candidates to find one right candidate, and he will leave a position unfilled if the inefficient "numbers game" does not yield the right worker. (Don't be surprised if an interviewer doesn't talk much about the job. He might be a cow himself. So help him out.)

No matter what anyone tells you, companies don't hire people in order to give them jobs. They hire people to get a job done. So don't do the interview. Do the job. A good hiring manager will notice the difference.

CHAPTER 6

Master Your Power

The Power of *Doing the Job*

A good attitude—one focused on the work to be done—is valuable only if it leads you to take action that benefits the employer. This is where most advice you've heard about interviewing falls flat on its face: it doesn't help you accomplish the transition from positive attitude to positive action. Instead, the employer and the candidate *talk* about a subject that just begs to see some action. You can talk yourself blue in the face without proving anything. Sometimes, you can confuse the heck out of the employer.

One employer posted this question on *Ask the Headhunter* on America Online:

> *How does a serious business select interview candidates who are legitimately seeking work? From past experience, there are many posers out there who think nothing of wasting employer time and resources when they are essentially satisfied with their present job and have no real interest in leaving. Can you offer any advice, profile or clues about applicants who are really only interviewing for the thrill?*

Actually, I don't think there are really many people who "interview for the thrill." But this manager was pointing out something very subtle about how most job hunters interview: they can't convince him that they really want the job. Most employers know there's something missing after all this talk (or "posing," as this manager puts it), but they can't tell you what it is. They regard lack of action on the part of the candidate as lack of interest in the job. The result is that a manager can't decide whether you're the right candidate. Sometimes, as in this case, the manager will wonder whether you're a "legitimate" candidate or a fraud—and all you're doing is "following the rules" of interviewing. Don't ever put yourself in this position.

Many job candidates can present an attitude powerful enough to get themselves in the door to interview, but they don't know how to translate that attitude into the action the manager needs to see. All they do is talk. They never take control of the interview, and that's where the power to impress an employer lies.

While many people are surprised to learn how much research it takes to prepare for an interview, they're even more surprised to hear me say that the job candidate can—and should—control the interview because he holds the real power. The source of that power is very simple: the employer needs some work done and you may be the only person who can do it the way he wants it done. This gives you power. Recognize this power and master it.

Remember: the manager needs you. Believe it or not, he *wants* you to be the last candidate he interviews. He *wants* you to be the best candidate for the job. Then he'll be able to hire you, stop interviewing, and get the job done.

> Your real power lies in being able to do the job a manager needs to have done. Cultivate and use that power!

Your power solidifies when you can answer "yes" to the Four Questions. This means your power depends on how much work and preparation you do to earn it. Recognizing that you are the solution to the employer's problem will help you to think of yourself as a consultant, not a candidate. You are not there to be interviewed, so you don't need to be nervous. You are there to understand a problem, and to *solve* it—not just to talk about it.

If you understand this power, you will realize that the outcome of any interview is up to you. Like Dorothy in *The Wizard of Oz*, you always have the power. But you must decide to use it. If you are prepared, qualified, and can handle the Four Questions, any interview should be a pleasure and *a win*. That is the power of doing the job.

Keep in mind that even a great interview may not result in a new job. You may learn in the interview that the job is not for you. Remember, the goal is not to get the job. The goal is to do the job. If you or the employer determines that you really cannot do the job or don't want to do the job, that's okay. Either iron out the differences or walk away from a relationship that isn't going to work. Sometimes you have to use your power to say no, or to acknowledge that a match is not right. You must act from a powerful position and do what is right for you and for the employer.

The Power of Information

We have talked a lot about the importance of preparation and finding the right answers to the Four Questions. You cannot prove you can do a job if you haven't studied a particular business and the people involved, as well as the work and its problems and challenges. To develop the power to do the job, you must first understand all these things. Ultimately, it is your knowledge that opens the door to a new job. This is the power of information.

To explore the power of information, I'm going to talk about three very important subjects that all too often get glossed over in the rush to find a job. First, and perhaps most important, I want to remind you that making choices is probably the most crucial aspect of your job search. There is just no way that you can acquire the in-depth information you're going to need about every job that comes along. *Which jobs you choose to learn about* is just as important as which jobs you actually pursue.

Second, I'm going to talk about the very messy business of figuring out what makes you tick—at least in your work life. I want to help you see that the quality of your future does not depend so much on finding a job as it does on figuring out what kind of work you want to do. Of course, you'll need a lot of information in order to accomplish this. Since I'm not a doctor, a therapist, or a counselor who claims to have specific answers, I'm just going to drop you into the middle of the biggest pile of information I know of and let you find your own way out. (Who said job hunting couldn't be fun?)

Finally, I'm going to show you where I have found the information I've used as a headhunter to match companies with candidates. Then I'm going to show you how you can use it to be your own headhunter.

The Importance of Making Choices

You must approach interviewing in a highly selective manner. This is important not only because you want to find the right job for yourself, but also because it takes a lot of work to uncover the information that will enable you to make a smart choice. There is just no way that you can research fifty companies in depth. My suggestion is to start with four or five target companies.

Most books about job hunting give you the opposite advice: go after as many companies as possible to increase your odds of getting someone's attention. Well, to me that's like trolling the local bars because you want to get married. Sure, you'll get some attention—but much of it will be the wrong kind of attention. Just because most of the action seems to be in the bars—or in the job classifieds—doesn't mean that it's the kind of action you're looking for. You will wind up rejecting most people who respond to you, and you run the risk of settling for less than you really want. Why? Because you're putting yourself into what's called a "forced choice" scenario. Rather than looking for the kind of relationship you really want, you settle for what seems to be available to you.

When you broadcast your availability, you stop making the important choices and you lose control of the outcome of your search. You can even turn some of your best prospects off, because they might prefer to be approached in an entirely different way. Nonetheless, people tend to broadcast because it's much easier than gathering the information that enables them to make real choices.

There are more wrong jobs out there for you than there are right jobs. You are a unique worker, with a special set of skills that can be very profitable for some employers—but not for just any employer. You must choose where you want to go. To make a smart choice, you must first gather the relevant information.

Here are your two basic choices: spend all your time sending out résumés to dozens of companies and going on lots of interviews, or spend most of your time carefully finding, researching, and preparing for the few jobs that are really right for you.

It continues to amaze me that people regard almost any "job opportunity" that's remotely connected to what they do as another possible job for them. In fact, all they're doing is letting themselves be distracted from the rich array of options that is actually open to them, if they're willing to make the effort to identify, explore, and pursue them.

Many people get frustrated if they're not out interviewing or distributing lots of résumés. But, they also become frustrated when nothing comes from their efforts. They don't feel in control when they go on interviews, but they wonder why they didn't receive an offer or why no one has called them.

The explanation is simple: if you don't expend the effort necessary to identify *where you want to go*, you'll never get there. It seems obvious, because we've all heard it before. But if you don't select interviews carefully, you can be certain you won't know enough about a job to even be talking about it, much less trying to demonstrate that you can do it. You will blow the interview. Why should anyone offer you the job? Why would you even want it? You will get what you put in: nothing. Don't wonder about it. Life is very simple, really. Do nothing, gain nothing.

You must offer value to get value. You must prepare to offer an employer a solution before he will offer you a job. And you can't create or deliver a solution unless you have made a conscious, informed choice about which jobs to tackle.

So, now that I've reminded you how important your power of choice is, how do you gather the information you'll need to help you make your first big choices?

Identify the Companies You Want to Work For

Ah, the real essence of the job search! The big choice! This is recognized as such a big issue that the employment industry has developed a special "for a fee" kind of "therapy" to help you with this nasty quagmire of indecision: it's called career counseling. The career doctor assesses your attitudes and your personality, pokes your intelligence, prods your aptitudes, and carefully extracts your painful wallet.* Then the good doctor—oops! *counselor*—gives you the results: a custom-tailored package of information that is basically a rehash of information he delivers to all his other patients—er, clients. (It's so easy to forget; the career doctor is not really a doctor.)

---

*If you find that changing jobs is producing serious emotional problems for you, or if you are depressed, frightened, or unusually anxious, you should probably talk with a psychological—not a career—counselor about what is troubling you. Job change is considered one of the most traumatic experiences of life. You should not hesitate to seek out professional help if you think you need it. But, don't put your psychological well-being in the hands of someone who has no credentials or expertise in the field of psychology, just because he calls himself a "counselor."

Let me save you some agony and lots of money, and while I'm at it, let me save you from the good intentions of your uncles, friends, and professional peers who all think they know just what kind of job you need. There is a good answer to the question *What jobs should I be going after?*

The answer, of course, is another question: *What do you want to do?*

Just as no one can tell you what you should order for dinner, no one can tell you which job to pursue. It's up to you. Listen to your appetite; listen to your interests; listen to your goals and aspirations. What companies thrill you? Where would you love to park your bike each day? What companies have you read or heard about that make you say "wow!"? What companies' products or services intrigue you?

Don't let someone else tell you where to spend most of your waking hours each day—figure it out for yourself, and make it good!

Don't let this decision scare you. Most people believe that this is the watershed event of their search. But it's not do-or-die, once you realize that your freedom to make choices doesn't end with the first choice. The great thing about making choices is that once you get good at it, your reward is that you get to make more of them!

What if a company I want to work for doesn't have any openings?

Call it "supply-side headhunting," but I've placed many people at client companies where there was no job available. Sometimes it happened because the person was so much "on the money" regarding the company's business that the company *created* a position for him. In other cases, when a job finally did open up, my candidate was the first one the company offered it to. In all cases, when a match was made it was because someone gathered and used the right information the right way.

What if I pick a company, and they don't hire me?

Well, you go on to the next. But you go on to the next one *of your choice.* In the meantime, you're spending your time profitably.

Rather than mailing out résumés to people you don't know who don't know you, you are studying a company at the level of detail that's necessary to make you an attractive, savvy job candidate. This is not something many people do. And that's precisely why companies don't hire most of the job candidates they interview: these candidates just don't *know* enough. They haven't bothered to gather, much less use, the information they need.

What if it turns out that the company I've settled on and researched just isn't right for me? Should I still go after them?

Absolutely not. Trust your own judgment. Drop that company off your list of four or five and add another one in its place. Don't be dismayed. When you make choices, you also learn from the consequences. Be satisfied that you pursued one dream until you reached its limits, and that you based your decision on good, hard information. Each time you drop a company, you will have learned more about how to better select the next one.

Now let me drop you into that big pile of information I mentioned earlier! This is where you learn to find the right employer by wandering around . . .

Start your search for the right company by spending some free-wheeling time at the library. The library is still one of the best sources of information known to man, woman, child, and headhunter. Among all this information there are *ideas* and there are *choices.* If you've never taken a day (or a week!) "off" just to roam the magazine racks and scan the stacks for books about topics that interest, motivate, stimulate, and excite you—do it! You're about to make a big decision in your life. Changing jobs is a challenge that requires you to think broadly rather than narrowly. Your mind needs room to explore, to think, to "blue sky." It needs to consider not specific jobs, but *possibilities.*

Psychologists talk about two kinds of basic problem-solving strategies. *Convergent thinking* is what happens when you bring all your cognitive faculties to bear on solving a problem. Reading the want ads is a convergent approach to job hunting. Going after a company you've targeted is also a convergent approach.

Divergent thinking involves working outward from the problem to find new ways of approaching it. Wandering in the library, seeking new ideas about what kinds of work you want to do, is a divergent approach to job hunting. Start your job search with divergent thinking! Enjoy exploring the possibilities! This is where you get to figure out what you want to do with the rest of your life (well, some of it, anyway), so that you can then focus on how to make it happen. *Don't worry about the "how" for now; concentrate on the "what."*

I can't tell you how many participants in my online *Ask the Headhunter* forum have written to say how they didn't realize—until after they'd spent thousands of dollars on career counseling—that most of the answers to their career questions were in the library. (By the way, if you find yourself getting lost in the library, go talk to The Keeper of All the Information—the reference librarian. Reference librarians are among my favorite people in the world because they know where all the information is and how to help you get your hands on it.)

You will quickly begin to see trends in your explorations—industries that you're attracted to, particular kinds of work and specific companies and businesses. Let yourself pursue your interests. Don't worry yet about "finding a job." Instead, investigate and learn about the kinds of work that get your juices flowing. If you find your interests are not matched by your skills, figure out whether you need more education. If you're confused—or inspired—by some of what you learn, find people who know more than you do and talk with them.

Do not avoid industries or companies that are "downsizing." Some of the best opportunities are in industries that are undergoing profound change. The media would have you believe that such change marks the end of an industry. Yet, the telecommunications industry isn't dying as AT&T is laying off thousands, and America doesn't stop manufacturing cars when General Motors encounters a downturn. In fact, these companies don't go out of business. They're *changing*, and they need your help.

You will begin to identify your target companies as you sift through information that matters to you. Drill down a step at a time. Start studying an industry first (this may be the one you're in, or it may be a new one). Move on to the various kinds of business done in that industry. Then study the individual companies—the ones that are driving the industry. Find out who the movers and shakers are: the people who determine where the industry and the key companies are going. Read about the prevalent issues the industry is facing, then drill down into the companies toward the people you would be working with. Get to know these people as if your next job depends on them, *because it does.*

As you wind your way through all this information, start a list of the companies and people you would love to work with. When you approach a company certain that you really want to work there, and knowing why, your confidence will make you a very powerful job candidate. Don't scratch your head and wonder if it's a pipe dream. Instead, decide if you're willing to tackle the next step toward the job you want. Then ferret out the specific information you'll need to wow the manager you want to work for.

The best way to impress the hiring manager is with your knowledge about him and his business. You know you're getting close to "wow" when the information you're gathering begins to reveal the problems and challenges a particular company is facing—and when you start developing ideas about how to solve them. This is how the headhunter coaches the right job candidate to walk into the interview and solve the manager's problems.

Now let's take a look at how the headhunter uses information to make things happen—and how you can use it to be your own headhunter.

Be Your Own Headhunter

To answer the Four Questions and to prepare yourself to do the job in the interview, you need to learn all you can about the specific industry, the specific company, and the specific people you want to work with. This is an information-hungry process, and you must feed it.

Start with the printed word (this includes information in electronic format, such as on the Internet and the World Wide Web).* Whether or not you realize it, there's lots to learn about the industry, the company, and the people you want to work with. Read it. Study it. Learn it inside out. Think about it. Practice talking about it. There is no substitute for knowing your quarry. Any shortcuts will leave holes in your knowledge, and these will weaken your power in the interview.

Expect to spend a week or so doing your research on an industry, and at least several days on each company. Don't let research become your new job—but do make sure that you're covering your subject in enough depth to make you feel comfortable about doing a presentation to the employer. I've seen people spend a good two weeks learning about their target; that's not unreasonable, depending on what you're trying to learn.

1. Finding information.

The information sources discussed below are essential when you're seeking a job in your own industry. They're absolutely critical when you're trying to enter a new industry. In the latter case, your skills, talents, and abilities may be transferable, but the context in which you will be applying them will likely be quite different. This is all the more reason to become as knowledgeable as you can be about the new industry. Start studying, thinking, asking questions, and developing profitable ideas. (Some of the information mentioned below may not be available on privately-owned companies because they are not legally required to divulge it. You

---

*I do not intend to provide a lesson in using the Internet. However, I strongly suggest that you learn how to use this ubiquitous communication technology. I have tried to set apart from the main text my specific suggestions about where to find relevant information on the Internet, so that if you choose to ignore this avenue (at your peril!) you may do so.

may need to dig harder to learn about companies whose stock is not publicly traded.)

1. *Company annual report:* This is a company's "slick" version of who they are, what business they are in, what they are good at, and what they think their prospects are. It also includes information about subsidiaries, divisions, executives, and lots of financial data. Call the company's corporate secretary and ask him to mail it to you. It's free.

2. *Company 10-K report:* The Securities and Exchange Commission (SEC) requires every public company to file a 10-K. This is the "brass tacks" version of the annual report and is also free. It includes certain information in a prescribed format. A company whose shares are openly traded on the stock exchange will send it to anyone who requests it. 10-K's are pretty easy to read, and they are more clearly organized than annual reports. They are especially useful because they discuss the company's competitors, strategic strengths and weaknesses, and problems it is facing. 10-K's also include biographies of key managers and information about their holdings in the company. The 10-K is a great source of high-level contacts. You will find it much more informative than the annual report. Order it at the same time you ask for the annual report. Compare the two.

3. *Company quarterly report and 10-Q:* Ask for the two most recent quarterly reports and 10-Q reports (the SEC "brass tacks" version), when you request the annual and 10-K reports. The quarterlies often provide detailed discussions about matters that aren't covered in much detail in the annual report. They're useful to help you understand what's been happening with the company in recent months.
World Wide Web: The SEC's EDGAR data base, which contains the SEC filings of publicly held corporations, is a quick and convenient way to access some of the above-mentioned

information, and more. You will also find that some companies distribute their reports electronically direct to interested parties via the Internet. This could save you a lot of time. (Don't let yourself get overwhelmed by the sheer amount of information you can gather online. Remember: you have a specific goal here. Focus on it.)

4. *Sales brochures:* Call the vice president of marketing's office and request literature about the company's major product lines. If you're asked why you want this information, explain that you're considering working for the company and you want to see where their product line stands in the industry. Or, say that you're considering purchasing stock, and you want to know more about the product lines. Also ask for brochures comparing the company's products with those of its competitors. Marketing departments commonly prepare such analyses for the benefit of their customers. The competitive information will also help you to learn about other companies. Call each of these in turn to learn even more. You will get a good idea about the state of the industry, and you will identify other potential employers.

World Wide Web: Most companies of any size (and many small ones, too) have Web sites. You can visit their online information databases with just a few clicks of your computer keyboard. These sites usually include plenty of promotional information and electronic product brochures. Much of this can be useful in your job search. On some sites, you will even find a way to communicate, via e-mail, with product managers and sales and technical staff. The very fact that you are using this progressive medium will often get you attention that you otherwise might not get. (Some companies also post job openings on their Web sites, or they provide electronic "employment forms." Be careful here. These are usually controlled by the human resources department. Everything I've said about dealing with human resources applies online as well as "off.")

Remember that all companies have competitors, and some of these competitors will have their own Web sites: more potential useful information—and contacts, and jobs—for you.

5. *Press releases and reprints of articles about the company:* Obtain these from the office of the vice president of marketing, customer relations, or corporate relations. Companies always have copies of press releases and favorable articles, which they give to their customers and investors. This will save you at least some time in the library. If you find one of the articles particularly useful, call the editor of the publication and ask whether they have written other articles about the company in the past year. You can even call the reporter who wrote the article. (This research technique is popular with headhunters.) Ask him any questions you might have, including who he interviewed for the article. Try to talk to those people. One of them could be your next boss. Be forthright. Don't be afraid to tell people that you're considering a job with the company and you're trying to learn all you can about it.

    World Wide Web: You can use one of the popular "search engines" on the Web to help you find the information you are seeking, from press releases to mentions of a particular company in online business directories and other publications. This is like having your very own reference librarian online. Alta Vista, a search engine developed by Digital Equipment Corporation, is accessible at [http://altavista.digital.com]. You can also try the Yahoo search engine at [http://www.yahoo.com]. Be careful, though. Merely requesting a search for all articles and references to "XYZ Corp." could turn up thousands of relevant pages of text. It's well worth learning how to use effective search techniques on the Web.

6. *Investment companies and analysts:* If you have a stockbroker, call him and request any research reports his firm has pro-

duced about your target company. Investment research firms, such as Standard & Poor, publish detailed analytical information on thousands of companies. You can find some of this at the public library; some of it might be available only at your broker's office. Ask for it.

World Wide Web: You can now find enormous amounts of analytical information about all sorts of companies online. You may have to pay for some of it. Dow Jones offers such reports at their *Wall Street Journal* site at [http://www.wsj. com]. The Motley Fool, the cutting-edge online analytical service that hosts my *Ask the Headhunter* forum, is both on the Web at [http://www.fool.com] and on America Online at keyword [fool]. The fool is especially useful because it will help you interpret—not just find—business information; and it's free.

7. *Business publications:* No matter what business you are in, you should subscribe to magazines like *Forbes, Business Week,* and *Fortune.* They contain a wealth of news and analytical information about thousands of companies. Scan all of them at the library for appropriate articles. I prefer *Forbes* because it provides frank editorial insights for investors and investigative articles about industries and companies. As a potential employee you are a potential investor. Advertisements are another source of valuable information. Most ads list a toll-free number you can call for information (many now list the company's World Wide Web address). Call and order whatever materials a company offers. For people with personal computers and modems, online information services are a must. There are lots of these today, including Microsoft Network, America Online, and Compuserve. These will provide you with their own brand of information, but they will also give you access to the Internet and the World Wide Web. (You can also open a direct Internet access account.) Investigate the business resources these easy-to-use online services offer, including corporate data

listings and the text of major business publications. Last but not least, do a computer search at the library. This will turn up useful articles and references.

World Wide Web: You can now find major newspapers and magazines published online. The *Wall Street Journal, New York Times, Washington Post, Boston Globe,* and *San Jose Mercury News* are just a few of the outstanding newspapers that offer you the ability to not just read the news, but also search it electronically for the subjects you're interested in. You will also find trade and industry journals online. One important bonus: many of these publications offer far more than articles. You will often find extended reporting included in the online edition; valuable information that the publication chose not to print because of space considerations, but which it can readily offer in this less costly electronic format.

8. *Biographies of key managers:* Some will be in the 10-K report. Follow up with *Who's Who* directories at the library, then do a computer search through periodicals for the names of those managers. These are people you can call for more information or for contacts. More important, this information will arm you properly for an interview with the company.

World Wide Web: Try using one of the search engines to look up references to a particular person at the company you're interested in. Digital's Alta Vista search engine is great for finding people by name. You will likely get many "hits" on names of executives. Other gems will turn up, too. For example, if a staff member of the company writes professional articles for industry publications, you might find information about them as well. These people may be more approachable, and you might have more to talk about if you contact them. I'm a big believer in calling executives, but the "grassroots" approach of talking to staff is an unbelievably productive way to learn what's really going on inside a company. It's also an excellent way to establish and build long-lasting contacts.

9. *Library reference guides:* Ask the reference librarian what he recommends to help you to research a particular company. Most local libraries have a reference hotline. Librarians are an underused information resource. Just ask for help. Don't be surprised if they offer to teach you how to use their computerized information databases!

10. *Trade journals and association directories:* There are myriad trade journals covering most industries that contain very detailed articles and "inside" information about various companies and industry issues. Before you can get your hands on these, you have to identify them. They can be pretty obscure. Trade journals are not always listed in a library's computerized indexes.

    One of the fastest ways to identify appropriate trade journals is to call a company on your target list. Ask the receptionist what trade journals the company subscribes to; there are probably several lying around in the company's reception area. If the receptionist is cooperative and the company is local, ask if you can stop by and pick up some old issues that were going to be discarded.

    Nonetheless, you can still start at the library. The reference librarian will help you find guides and directories listing professional associations for the industry you are interested in. Call one of these associations and ask what publications report on that industry. Also ask for a list of the association's members. There might be a charge for a directory, but it can be a gold mine of information. Association directories are one of my favorite information sources. The association may also publish a newsletter. Request sample copies whenever you can.

    There are also directories of professional publications at the library that list most, if not all, of the professional journals published. However, when using one of these directories, it's often hard to determine which journals are the important ones. That's why my favorite method for finding the best journals is to talk to a representative company.

If you can't find copies of appropriate trade publications in the library (I'll bet you'll find very few), call the publication directly and ask for a complimentary copy of a recent issue. Your efforts will be worth it. Look through the journals and publications you obtain. Often, articles are tagged with author biographies. An author may work for a company you're researching. Use the author as a source. Call him to learn more about his work, about job opportunities, and to get names of department heads at his company. Journal authors are very valuable sources for a headhunter. They are typically very visible in their industries and they have excellent contacts.

It's no coincidence that most of the information gathering I've been describing will lead you to human beings: employees of a company, vendors who sell to it, competitors, customers, reporters, fellow association members. These are the people a headhunter turns to when he's trying to find the right candidate for one of his clients. They are the same people who can lead you to the right hiring manager.

Keep two things in mind: information is useless unless it leads you to the right hiring manager; and, once you get to the right manager, you must have the right information at your fingertips, or he won't give you the time of day.

Now, what do you do with all the research you've done? Use it to help answer the Four Questions, so that you can decide whether to pursue a job at a particular company. Use it to lay a foundation for discussions you're going to have with people who already work with your target company—that's how you position yourself to learn even more from them. Finally, use it to convince the manager you've targeted that he should want you on his team. This is how you become your own headhunter.

2. Gathering inside information.

Don't let yourself get too wrapped up in research at the library, with your head buried in journals and directories. The point of that kind of research is to get you on the phone talking with the right people—ultimately, with the manager who's going to hire you. It only takes one or two cooperative contacts to get you on the right track.

Start by talking with people who work with the manager, then make your way up to the manager himself. The purpose for taking a slightly winding course to get to the person who would hire you is twofold. First, you want to gather more inside information so you'll have something to say to the manager when you finally reach him. The best source is the people who work with him. Second, the peripheral people you talk with are in a great position to introduce you to the manager. That's far better than calling him cold. The manager is more likely to talk with someone his team already knows than a complete outsider.

You often acquire very valuable "inside information" about a job from other employees in the company. That's why it's crucial to develop inside contacts who will share it with you. You might be able to get the name of a contact from a trade publication, a friend, or another company that does business with your target. A company salesperson is usually very easy to reach: there's no effort to keep you away from them, and they usually answer their own phones. Salespeople tend to appreciate how frustrating it can be to reach the right person in an organization; it's their job.

When you reach a sales rep, be ready to talk about the product. Then shift the discussion to getting a little advice:

> *Hi, my name is Mike Frey. I've been using your Bixtron Widget and I think it's a great product. I'd like to talk to someone in your design department about some ideas I've got for some features you ought to add to it. Who should I talk with about that? . . . Should I call back or can you connect me?*

If you can get the sales rep to connect you to someone in design (or whatever department it is you want to work in), introduce yourself. Start by talking a little about the product and the company. But then you can be a little more blunt. Explain that you're trying

133

to learn more about new job opportunities *in that specific department*. Don't let anyone push you off to personnel.

> *I want to get an accurate idea of opportunities in the* [department name] *department from a real employee. Can you give me some advice about how to do that, without talking to the personnel department? Is there someone you would suggest I talk with?*

You'll be surprised at how much information people are willing to share about their employers. Some will share because they love their company and want to tell the world. Some will share because they're frustrated and need someone to complain to. Be careful about how you interpret such judgments. Get enough information to form your own opinions.

Don't interrogate the person you reach. Have a conversation. Share some positive news you might have read about the company. Ask your contact if he can add any details. Ask about a specific job, whether there are any open jobs you should know about, or about upcoming opportunities in general. *Get the name of the manager who would most likely have an open position.*

As a rule of thumb, avoid calling a personnel department. They may have information you can use, but they can also cripple your efforts. Personnel jockeys are known for saying things like "I don't want you bothering the manager, or other employees, with phone calls and questions. All your contact must be with me." If the personnel department finds out you subsequently called a hiring manager, your efforts could drown in bureaucratic hot water. Personnel can't hire you (unless you work in personnel), but through all sorts of administrative mechanisms they can prevent a manager from hiring you or talking with you. So be careful about opening that Pandora's box.

3. Getting on the phone.

Here are some telephone tactics I have used as a headhunter, presented in a way that will help you to use them as a job hunter.

They can be applied with some modification to situations where you're doing preliminary research on a company (to find out what jobs might need doing), or if you have an interview scheduled and are trying to do some homework beforehand.

USING SCRIPTS

If you hate talking on the phone with strangers, take the advice of someone who was forced to learn to do it. When I first became a headhunter, I had to cold-call dozens of people each day to establish my initial contacts in the electronics industry. (I am still in touch with quite a few of these original contacts.) It was brutal and I froze whenever someone answered the phone. To solve this problem, I wrote out some scripts that would get me through the first awkward moments of a call.

Your scripts should be just long enough to get a call started and keep it on track. Create as many scripts as you think you need for various kinds of calls. Just be sure to practice them out loud before you use them. There's nothing worse than getting a call from someone who is obviously reading to you on the phone. Make your scripts conversational. Call a few friends and test them out.

Here's an example of a script for someone who is looking for a design job. Let's say you just got through to a company's design department, and you're trying to get information about a job in design.

Hi. My name is Mike Frey. I was just talking with Joe in sales about your Bixtron Widget. I've really gotten a lot of use out of that Widget. But I'd like to suggest that you use a more powerful spring on the lever. Do you think that would make it more powerful? . . . You know, the more I learn about your products, the more interested I get in the company in general. I've been very successful here, but I'd love to know more about the Widget industry. I've also been considering a move to Illinois [or wherever this company is located]. *Can you give me a little advice? What's it like to work there at Bixtron? Do you deal much with design yourself? Is there someone who you think might be willing*

135

to tell me what it's like to work in Bixtron's product design department? No, I really don't want to talk with personnel. I'd like to get a little perspective from a design expert in your business. . . . Anyway, thanks for the advice about how to get more force out of that handle.

You obviously want to leave room for discussion; don't just run through all those words willy-nilly. In fact, you want the other person to do most of the talking, and that script is way too long. You'll need to pick and choose the parts that will make it easy for the listener to talk to you. Tailor it into your own script. Nonetheless, it should give you some ideas about how to try and structure a call. The point is to get the other person to talk and share information with you. In particular, you want him to give you a name or to connect you with someone who does the kind of work you want to do.

Here's another approach. This is a simple, nonthreatening referral request you can make of just about anyone you reach at the company. Call a person at the company whom your research indicates might be a source of information. (Try to write your own script for this one.) Introduce yourself briefly, and state what kind of work you do. Finish up with: *"Can you tell me whose department is responsible for this kind of work?"* Note that the question is phrased in a way that will get you the name of a manager rather than just the name of a department. Make sure you get a name.

If you are directed to the personnel office, try this: *"Thanks, but my questions are very specific. I want to talk with someone who works in* [production, marketing, or whatever work you do] *and who specializes in* [the work you do]."

Once you have a name, you're in.

GETTING PAST THE RECEPTIONIST

It's always best to ask for a specific person when you call a prospective employer. This is true whether you're trying to reach the manager you'd be working for, or some other manager who might serve as your connection to him. If you've done your homework and read up on subjects that are of mutual interest to you and the manager, when he answers, you'll have something to talk about.

If the manager's secretary answers, you're also in good shape. When you're asked what you want to talk to the manager about, rely on your research and your new common interests with the manager:

I'm Mike Frey over at Western Equipment. I was just reading about Tom's work in Widget Monthly. *Nancy Weston, who wrote the article, suggested I give Tom a call to find out how he managed to get quality and yields up so high. He did an incredible job.*

There's almost nothing the secretary could do to screen that call. You're another professional calling to talk to his boss about his business. At worst, he could connect you with someone on Tom's staff who might be able to answer your questions. But then you have an inside line to Tom's department.

So, let's get to the hard part. How do you get past the company's main receptionist who answers the phone?

When you don't know the name of the manager of the department you want, call the main company number and ask who is in charge of the department. You're looking for a *name.* If you get it, ask to be connected. Some receptionists will be quite cooperative, but many receptionists are instructed not to reveal this information, for fear that a headhunter like me is trying to recruit employees. If the receptionist isn't cooperative, say "thank you" and hang up. Don't give your name or leave a message. Wait a while (a day, if possible) and call back.

This time, try to get connected to the *department* you want: "Hi. Marketing [or whatever department it is you want], please." Don't sound too friendly and don't sound lost. Your tone should make you appear businesslike, firm, and in a bit of a rush (otherwise you'll stand out from the other typical calls and you might make the receptionist pause to think about what you're really doing). When you get through, you will be talking with a departmental receptionist or a staff member. Ask for the name of the department manager. If no one will put you through, say, "Thanks anyway" and hang up.

Now you'll feel a little frustrated. How do you get through? If the above approaches don't work, your final tactic will be a little more aggressive. Ask the receptionist for the customer service or sales department. You won't be asked for a name, but you might be asked what part of the country you're calling from (a company's sales and service functions are usually broken up by region, and so are the people responsible for them). No receptionist will deny you access to sales or service. When you get connected, ask to be transferred: *"Oh, this is customer service? I wanted marketing. Sorry about that. Can you patch me through to the marketing department? By the way, who heads up marketing?"* Sure, this is stretching things a little. It may be the receptionist's job to keep you away from your target, but yours is to plow through. When you get the name you need, call that person directly. Do your homework, and try the script described above if you reach the manager's secretary.

4. Talking with the hiring manager.

The ultimate inside information always comes from the source of the job. Eventually, you will get to the manager in charge of the department in which you think you are interested. Make sure you're prepared to have an intelligent discussion with the manager about his work. Hopefully, you were able to get yourself introduced by someone the manager knows well. The best scenario is to have the contact suggest to the manager that you're the kind of person he should consider hiring.

If you have developed a particularly good contact who can introduce you, have the contact coordinate an in-person meeting if he can. This might even be a visit to your contact's office, followed by a walk down the hall to casually meet the manager. My preferred introduction happens over lunch—suggest that you all go down to the company cafeteria for a sandwich.

Whether your discussion with the manager involves another

party, and whether it's on the phone or in person, your goal is to establish yourself as a peer with common interests. This relationship—usually enjoyed by headhunters—will position you to prove that you can help the manager. At this point, he is not a prospective employer, but a source of information (he just happens to be the ultimate source). So, don't worry about the job. If you can accomplish what I'm suggesting, you will have plenty of opportunity to talk about that later.

The research you did prior to this meeting will have provided you with lots to talk about. Take the opportunity to compliment the manager about something positive you may have read or heard about his work. Engage him in a discussion about it. Ask his opinion about the state of the industry. Offer your thoughts. Ask for his advice.

If you think you're ready, express your interest in the work his team is doing. Keeping in mind what you uncovered in your research about the problems and challenges he's probably facing, be ready to suggest how you could contribute to his team's success. If you get the discussion going in this direction, you're in an interview. Prepare to demonstrate how you're going to do the job!

5. Preparing for the interview.

Your final—and most important—information-gathering effort will be one you must make just before your interview. Your goal is to talk with the manager before that critical meeting and to gather the most specific information possible about the work you would be hired to do. In other words, what problems and challenges would he want you to tackle? This will provide you with the material for your presentation.

LEARNING FROM THE MANAGER

If you already have an interview scheduled with the company, call the manager. Explain that you are preparing for your *meeting*. Don't use the word *interview*. Put him on track to view this as a *working meeting* rather than a traditional question-and-answer session. Introduce (or, hopefully, reintroduce) yourself and confirm your meeting date and time. Then jump-start your interview:

> *I look forward to meeting you. When I come to this kind of meeting, I treat it with the same respect I reserve for my first day on the job—I like to be ready to do the work. I want to be prepared to show you how I do the work that matters most to you. What's the biggest challenge you foresee for the person you're going to hire to do this job?*

The manager should be willing to spend a little time to explain the work to you and to tell you about his department. However, some managers prefer to wait until the interview to talk about a job, because they don't want to explain it all twice—on the phone and later again in the interview. It can help to point out that you share the interviewer's goal: *"I want to help make our meeting as productive as possible, without wasting any of your time. I want to be ready to show you exactly how I would do the job you need to have done."*

If you have decided on this approach, then suggest doing a brief presentation to the manager during the interview (see "Do the Job During the Interview" in chapter 4).

LEARNING FROM THE MANAGER'S ASSISTANT

If you can't reach the manager prior to your interview, talk with his secretary or administrative assistant. This person will likely have some information that will be useful to you. Be polite. Treat the assistant the way you would treat the manager. Explain that you have an interview coming up and that you want to make the meeting as productive as possible. Ask if the assistant can tell you a little about the job or about the manager. Have your questions ready, organized from the most general to the most specific, but start with the general ones. Get as many answered as you can. Explain that the more prepared you are, the more organized your meeting with the manager will be, and that you want to avoid taking up more time than necessary.

Many assistants are glad to help make their boss's meetings more productive, as long as they're not breaching confidentiality. If you feel bold, make the call and see what you come up with. If you get cold feet once you're on the phone, use the call to confirm your meeting time, then at least ask whether the assistant can offer any advice about how you can prepare for a good meeting with the manager.

Any information that anyone gives you in the course of your search can be valuable. So, treat a source of information like someone who is giving you a gift—because that's exactly what they're doing. Be grateful. Be respectful. Always say "thank you." When someone gives you something of value, remember to return the value. You may not be able to do a favor for that specific person, but you "owe" the favor to the pool of friendly people in the world. Remember to do a favor for someone else who needs it, whoever it might be. What goes around comes around. Participate in and promote the cycle.

Profit from Your Information

When you start exploring the world of information, let yourself dig very deeply at first. Investigate the various sources. Learn what research methods are most efficient for you. *Take time to develop a system of your own for gathering information.* Learn to mold the information you gather into knowledge that you can use to help your target employer. Always present what you've learned in that context. Then select from the methods I've discussed the ones that work best for you. The investment you make in learning to find important information will pay off now, and it will pay off in other ways later, once you are on the job.

Don't let all these sources of information overwhelm you. Take comfort in the fact that more information exists than you will ever be able to gather or use. But also take heed: the fact that this information exists means that others can use it to win the job you want. Cows won't bother. But not all your competitors are cows. And some of them are headhunters.

SUMMARY OF INFORMATION SOURCES

Here is a list of information sources discussed in this book. You can access much of this information on the Internet or various online services. As you start searching, you will discover many more sources of your own.

INFORMATION YOU CAN READ

- Company annual report
- Company quarterly report
- Company 10-K & 10-Q reports
- Company press releases
- Sales, product, & services brochures
- Advertisements
- *Forbes*
- *Fortune*
- *Business Week*
- *Wall Street Journal*
- *Barron's*
- *The Motley Fool*

- *Standard & Poor's Stock Reports*
- SEC EDGAR Database
- Local library reference desk
- Reprints of articles
- *Who's Who* directories
- Business directories
- Industry associations
- Industry association member directories
- Industry trade journals
- Directory of associations
- Industry newsletters

PEOPLE YOU CAN TALK TO

- Managers
- Secretaries / administrative assistants
- Company salespeople
- Other company employees
- Customers of the company

- Competitors of the company
- Vendors / distributors to the company
- Reporters at trade journals
- Editors & authors of articles
- Heads of industry associations

The Power of the Offer

You might expect that the subject of how to handle an offer would come at the very end of a book about how to win a job. But the job offer is not something you should think about only at the end of your job search. It is crucial that you understand your options once an offer is made, but you must consider the nature of these options at the beginning of your search—otherwise, you won't be able to prepare to negotiate the best offer you can get.

The final power in the job hunter–employer relationship lies in the job offer. This is a power few people realize they have when they receive a job offer. If you have used information effectively, and you proved you can do the job, the ultimate outcome of your job search will depend on how you exercise the power of the offer. At the outset, the employer controls the offer and the power it represents. Upon making the offer to the candidate, the employer transfers its power as well.

If you can understand the job and demonstrate that you can do it, you will be in a very good position to win an offer. You will win it because you showed respect for the manager's goal of *getting the job done* by successfully doing the job in the interview. Once you have the offer, you have the power to decide what happens next.

Although it is not the focus of this book, it is worth pointing out that many candidates run into the worst problems right after they receive an offer. They become so excited that they grab the offer and run. They don't stop to consider the power they wield.

> As far as the candidate is concerned, having an offer and knowing what to do with it requires at least as much control and presence of mind as winning the offer. This is the point at which things really start to happen *if the candidate uses his power*.

Once you have an offer, the ball is finally in your court. Now you can legitimately start trying to decide whether you really want the job. You have successfully addressed the employer's goals. Now you can start asking the questions that will help you achieve *your* goal, whether that goal is a certain level of responsibility, a certain amount of money, or the freedom to do the job a certain way.

The concepts we have talked about have come together to put the power in your hands. Enjoy your achievement. Whether you ultimately accept the job or not, you have reached an important goal: you proved you can do the job, and you have earned the privilege to do the job.

Exercise your power to negotiate what you want before you act to accept the offer. In fact, this is the time for you to explore *changing the offer* to suit your goals and to fully interview the company. Ask questions about any matters that concern you. You have earned the right to focus on *your goals.* You can exercise these prerogatives during either the meeting in which you were given the offer or a subsequent meeting.

> My suggestion is to separate the winning of the offer from the negotiation of its terms. Schedule a separate meeting.

You should have your offer in writing. If it is not in writing, tell the manager you will need it in writing before you can consider leaving your present job. It is desirable to receive a verbal offer at the end of an interview, but the written offer is what counts. Make sure you have the entire package, including a description of benefits, the company employee handbook, and so on.

> Never resign your current job or make any irrevocable plans or decisions before you have an offer in writing.

Companies rescind offers on occasion, although I have seen it happen *very* rarely. The consequences can be dire for the job hunter. Companies find it much more difficult to rescind an offer that has been made in writing because their legal (not to mention ethical) exposure is greater.

Thank the interviewer for the offer; tell him you are very pleased to receive it and that you are excited about the prospect of working with him. Look him in the eye when you say this.

Review the Offer

Resist the temptation to accept the offer on the spot. You don't know what the offer really is until you read the fine print. Explain that you would like a little time to review the offer, including the salary, benefits, bonus, and retirement plan. Decide in advance of your interview how much time you will need to consider an offer. A manager who makes you an offer deserves a specific decision date that you will adhere to.

Your answer date should be dependent on receipt of the *written* offer. For example, don't promise an answer three days after the date of the verbal offer. Promise an answer three days after you receive the written offer. Tell the manager that when you receive it, you'll call and confirm that it arrived. If the personnel department is responsible for mailing out offers, this may take longer than he thinks. The issue here is that written offers sometimes contain surprises relating to things you haven't thought much about. For example, there might be a restrictive non-compete clause or an unusual limitation on health insurance. You don't want to accept a verbal offer, only to have to reopen a negotiation about the written details afterward.

Now, go kick up your heels, congratulate yourself, and think about the offer. Then think about what else you need to know about the company and the job. Is there any aspect of the offer you would like to negotiate before making a decision?

Interview the Company

Before the decision date you have agreed to, call the manager and tell him you feel good about the offer, but you would like to meet with him one more time to gather a little more information that is important to you. Don't let this meeting happen over the phone. Do it in person.

The power you hold in the time between the offer and your acceptance is not a license to act irresponsibly. To do so could cost you the offer (the company could withdraw it if they're not happy with changes you suggest). It could also color the manager's attitude toward you after you begin work. However, it would be just as irresponsible to enter a work relationship that is not right for you. You've worked hard to get this far. Take this period between the offer and your acceptance (or refusal) as an opportunity to make sure you're putting your life on a new, healthy path. Make sure you're satisfied with the path.

Some employers will be a little surprised that you have requested a follow-up meeting. But such meetings are common when a headhunter is involved. Often the headhunter serves as the go-between, gathering and delivering more detailed information, and negotiating the fine points. Don't let yourself be intimidated by that piece of paper. Don't let yourself think that a good company would become easily upset because you want to talk things over a little more. If you find resistance, it will likely be for bureaucratic reasons (e.g., personnel policies and expectations). Make sure you're talking with the hiring manager, and make sure you're friendly and oriented toward making a good match. The employer has invested a lot to find you and make you an offer; he won't easily let you go. Be reasonable, but be firm.

Here is a sampling of requests job candidates rarely make that you can bring up after an offer has been extended, if you have not brought them up during the interview.* Think of some of your own. However, don't overwhelm the employer. Ask only the questions that are most important to you.

*It's usually best to hold off on some of these questions until after you receive an offer. For example, employers who like to conduct very traditional interviews may feel put off by being asked to introduce other company employees into the interview process. Or, due to schedule constraints, they may not have time to give you a facility tour or show you the tools used in their department. Use your judgment on this point, but don't fail to get the information you need before you accept an offer.

- *Your team:* Ask to meet members of the team you have been invited to join. Make sure they are people with whom you want to work.
- *Other influences:* Ask to meet the managers and important staff members in other departments who will affect your ability to do your job. Interview them, because your success will depend on them.
- *The tools:* Ask to see all the tools that will be at your disposal. If you don't think they are sufficient for you to do your job properly, request the tools you will need now, because it will be more difficult to get them later. (Tools may be physical or intangible ones.)
- *Structure:* Ask about the organizational structure and find out how it impacts your job. Who is your boss's boss? What is the normal career path for the job? How have people migrated through the organization structure? Does your boss plan to be in his job for the next year? (You don't want to take the job only to find that in a month you are reporting to someone you've never met.)
- *The job:* Suggest changes to the job now, before you accept it, if you believe the changes will materially affect your ability to perform the job most profitably. *Do the company a favor, and be its consultant before you become its employee.*
- *Compensation:* Negotiate for more money, if you think it's truly warranted. You must believe you are worth any additional money you ask for, and you must be ready to explain why. Be forthright about it, and present your explanation in terms of your value to the company. Remember that money comes in different forms: salary, starting bonuses, guaranteed first raise, performance bonuses, incentives, merit raises, stock options, stock grants, pension plans and 401(k) contributions, loans, moving expenses, computer equipment to use at home, medical benefits, paid vacation time (and unpaid vacation time), a car allowance, and tuition reimbursement, to name a few. There are many ways to get what you want; always have alternatives you're

ready to accept if the company won't agree to a particular request.

- *Review schedule:* Negotiate your performance review schedule, both in terms of promotion and in terms of salary increases or bonuses. Ask for guarantees, especially in the first year, if you think it's warranted.

Postoffer negotiations not only serve you well, but also reveal to a good manager that you understand the factors that will affect your success at the job. Your success is his success. Take the time to write out your specific questions and requests before you schedule this follow-up meeting with the manager. Talk to a trusted friend or mentor to review your requests to make sure they're reasonable.

If It's Important, Ask for It

Review the positives and negatives about the offer, the job, your boss, your coworkers, your career path, and the company. Two columns on a page still work best: label one (+) and one (−).

If you find more negatives than you are comfortable with, don't despair. I have often successfully negotiated issues that I thought would be deal breakers. You might be surprised what an employer will agree to, if you ask for it in a reasonable manner, and with an eye to the employer's interests as well as your own.

Make a list of what would have to be changed, either about the offer or the job, to make you happy. (Be realistic; don't ask for use of the corporate jet unless you really think you will need it.) It is perfectly legitimate to present your requests to the manager you would be working for. He doesn't have to accede to them, but if these things are critical to you, you'd better put your concerns out on the table now. You have not won in this job hunting enterprise unless you have the job you want, with good compensation, under satisfactory conditions. As long as your requests are reasonable, you will learn a lot about how flexible the company is, and how seriously it will take future requests from you.

If a company has a terribly negative reaction to your bringing these subjects up at this time, you have some decisions to make. Are you willing to concede important points *permanently*? If you don't negotiate these points now, are you willing to live with the possibility they will never get addressed *after* you start the job? Will these issues hurt you later if you take the job? Is the company looking for a worker who can contribute to change and growth, or does it want a robot that will move its hands and feet and keep its mouth shut?

Consider these things before you accept the offer, because the only option you will have later will be to resign if you don't like what you find. It's easier to negotiate a new job than it is to negotiate a position after you've accepted it. Finally, remember that if it's not in writing, it's open to interpretation at a later date.

Negotiate Your Terms

This is the power of the offer. Potent, isn't it? Most people never put it to use.

You have earned the power to do all these things after you receive an offer because you have *done the job*. You have met the employer's needs. Don't fret about how the employer might react to your requests. The fact that you have an offer in your hands is proof that the company needs and wants you. As long as you present your requests professionally and not as demands, and they are reasonable and realistic and clearly reflect your desire to *equally ensure your success and the company's success*, a good company will consider the things that are important to you because they want to hire an employee who is satisfied and motivated to produce his best work.

Use your power to negotiate for your goals and to decide whether, and on what terms, you want to "hire the company" as your employer.

CHAPTER 7

New Interview Instructions

Before the Interview: Doing the Down-and-Dirty

When you think about preparing for an interview, stop and think first about preparing for the job. If you have prepared yourself to do a job, you will be ready to talk about it in a meeting with an employer. This is the down-and-dirty part of getting ready. It doesn't have to be painful, if you recognize it as a good time to assess who you are, what you can do, what you want, and what you have to offer.

The following guidelines will help to keep you on track as you begin your job search. If you think about it carefully, you will see that each item in some way contributes to helping you answer one or more of the Four Questions.

1. Know what you can do, and be ready to talk about it.

Take a piece of paper and list what you do (simply, so your grandmother would understand it!). Avoid using complicated terms or industry jargon. What are the essentials of the work you do every day? What are your skills? What is your expertise? "Worksheet 6: What Is Your Value?" will help you with this (see chapter 4).

If you find these questions difficult to answer, try this approach. Step out of your shoes. Look at these questions from your current employer's practical point of view. This is the view other employers will have when they meet with you. Think about the work you do this way: What does your employer *pay you to accomplish*? Have you accomplished it? How? Using what tools?

Next, learn to communicate this information effectively. Practice your delivery two ways. First, try explaining it to someone from your industry who understands what you do and who can offer useful "insider" suggestions and criticism. Then practice describing it to a friend who knows you but doesn't really understand what you do. Be very clear. Don't turn your presentation into a lecture: allow it to change and evolve each time you talk about it.

If you make it a very structured presentation, you will feel stiff in an interview. You will also find that the more "formal" you make it, the easier it will be to forget entire parts of it. This will just make you nervous. Say it the way you normally talk. Make sure you leave room for discussion, because presenting it in one fell swoop can make it difficult to have a conversation with the interviewer. Make it easy for the interviewer to interrupt you and focus on details that are important to him.

Don't get so involved in your presentation that you aren't *listening*, too. The interviewer will have things to say. Make sure you *hear* him, and that you can engage in a useful discussion.

If you think that I'm trying to help you keep your presentation at the level of a casual discussion, you're right. You must be informative, but you should avoid giving a speech. Imagine sitting down with your boss to plan the way you're going to tackle a project. Have the same kind of confidence in the interview. Remember: you've already done this sort of thing many times at your job.

In your practice presentations, take note of the kinds of questions your friend asks; use them to polish your explanation. Then sit down and write a detailed outline describing what you do. Refer to "Do the Job During the Interview" in chapter 4. By now, you should be clear and articulate when talking about your work—and you should be comfortable discussing it with any employer.

2. Which companies need your skills the most?

Identify general categories first: manufacturing or service companies, high-tech or low-tech companies, small or big companies. Then go to the library and find directories listing those kinds of companies. Ask the reference librarian to help you.

Look in the Sunday editions of major newspapers like the *New York Times, Los Angeles Times, San Jose Mercury News, Washington Post,* and *Boston Globe;* these papers don't have to be current. Find an edition of the *Wall Street Journal* with classified ads focused on your industry. Read through the employment ads carefully and start listing companies by industry.* Don't become too caught up in the ads themselves—you're not using the newspaper to find a job.

If you have a computer, explore the online services. Most of them publish extensive information about American businesses, companies, and jobs. Take advantage of the World Wide Web. On the Motley Fool alone you will find detailed information on over two thousand companies.

When you're done with these sources of information, you should have a list of industries and companies in which you are interested. Check off the industries and companies that are likely to have job functions where your skills would be of use. Refer to your "what I do" outline (from worksheet 6 in chapter 4) and shorten the list further to include those companies you believe would actually benefit from your skills. Finally, break these down by geography, depending on where you want to live (or where you're willing to relocate).

The next cut is done by "feel." You must decide, based on your interests and inclinations, which of the remaining companies may be worth detailed research. Don't restrict yourself too much when making this cut. This is the time to chase some of your dreams. Robert Browning said, "A man's reach should exceed his grasp." Go for it.

---

* This exercise is not intended to encourage you to start using the want ads to find a job, just to show you a couple of ways to explore industries and companies that might benefit from your skills. The want ads represent a wonderful database describing the kinds of businesses and work that exist in our country.

Don't be overwhelmed by all the industries and companies you have identified. The possibilities will seem staggering because they *are*. But remember, among all those possibilities, you need to find only *one* job. You will find it.

Now comes the hard part. You have developed a list of possible employers. You need to gather as much information as you can about each of these companies. Refer to "The Power of Information" in chapter 6 for ideas about how to find it. The information you gather will help you to identify specific companies that could profit from your skills. When you are done, you should have a short list of companies you think you want to work for, and which might have jobs you can and want to do. Whether or not you saw ads for such jobs is irrelevant. Don't be dismayed even if your research revealed that a company you're interested in is not currently hiring. I have done many searches for companies that claimed publicly they were not hiring.

3. Does a particular company have a job for you?

Not just a *job*, but a job *for you*. This is grueling research, because you are trying to be smarter than the employer. You are trying to identify compelling reasons why a company needs you, before it has come to that conclusion itself. This is why I say you should not let it become an employer's responsibility to determine whether you are qualified to do a particular job. If you take the initiative to prove to an employer that he needs you, you will earn an interview and be well on your way to an offer before you even go to the interview. *That is the kind of candidate an employer is waiting for.* You have to learn everything there is to be learned about the company, and you have to sit down and map out how your skills fit into the company's profile. Use the information-gathering techniques discussed in "The Power of Information" in chapter 6.

Ask yourself how you can help the company achieve its goals. This sounds lofty, but it is a question the members of the company's board of directors ask themselves every time they meet. (I firmly believe that anyone who doesn't regularly think about this issue is doing both his employer and himself a disservice.) Do your research by talking to company employees, the company's customers, its suppliers, and industry groups to which it belongs. Find someone at the company who has time to educate you about who they are, what they do, and what they need. You have to work to ferret out this important information.

When you start talking to the right people, something magic will happen: you will learn about good jobs that need to be filled, and you will begin getting referrals, introductions, and recommendations from people who know the company well.

4. Figure out what the job really is.

Every job has a formal, written description—and then there's what the job is *really* all about. Most job descriptions are jargon-filled bureaucratese written by personnel jockeys, and they're not very accurate. But suppose you could get a look at such a job description before your interview. Would it benefit you? I can almost guarantee that when you meet with the manager of the job, you will find that his description of what he wants you to do is considerably different from what the personnel jockey told you. Always try to get the story from the source.

The only person who can give you a good idea about what the job will involve long-term is the manager who's going to hire you. Don't wait until the interview to learn what a job is really about, and don't expect to learn it from an ad.

But be careful; sometimes even a manager cannot tell you exactly what he wants. He's trying to follow the rules of the traditional interview, and bluntness is not one of the rules. Now what do you do? How do you find out what the job is *really all about*?

The headhunter has a distinct point of view about this question that you should always keep in mind:

> Every job actually has the same description: *earn more profit for the employer.* That's it. The employer created this job to generate more profit. To understand what a particular manager is looking for in a job candidate, you must figure out *what it is about this job that earns more profit for the company.*

How will the worker who does this job produce profit for the company, day after day, week after week? You have to figure this out by talking with people and by learning as much as you can about the company. You have to think about the company's business and wonder why this job even exists. No one outside the company can do this for you. There are no books or "experts" who can tell you. The closer you come to answering this question, the more the manager will want to talk with you.

So, start doing some research and start doing a lot of thinking. Even if the conclusion you come to is not entirely correct, you will be well on the way toward knowing what to discuss in your interview. The employer will see the difference between you and the last cow he interviewed.

5. Let the company know you exist.

Employers are more likely to hire insiders. You have to become an insider rather than a job applicant. Don't go into the company anonymously. An unsolicited résumé is not the best introduction. Why? Because when an employer looks at it, he is not looking at you. Your résumé is like an ad for a used car, and there are thousands of those in the newspaper. Most of them are alike. Why should he look at yours?

Calling the personnel department is also a poor way to start, unless you're looking for a job in personnel.

Sending your résumé in response to ads is more likely to get you into a black hole than into a job. Suppose you're a shoemaker, who is applying for a job with a shoe company. If someone in marketing gets your résumé, decides you're not marketing material, puts an X on it, and sends it to personnel for filing, you're doomed. When the shoemaking department calls personnel with a job opening, all personnel knows is that your résumé has a big X on it. You've been sucked into a black hole.

This happens all the time. More than once I've enjoyed the experience of placing a qualified worker at a company that already had his résumé. Personnel didn't know they had the résumé; it was buried in their files. The right hiring managers never saw it. On these occasions, companies were paying me large fees to find job candidates who were already "on file"—in the black hole.

The way to let a company know you exist is much simpler than all this useless paper pushing. How do you win a date with someone you're interested in? Either you ask the person directly, or you make the object of your desire want to go out with *you*. Decide which manager you think you want to work for and call him. Better yet, have someone else put the bug about you in the manager's ear, just as you might have a mutual friend try to set you up with a date.

Don't be an anonymous candidate waving his hand in the crowd. Get yourself introduced to the company by someone the company knows and respects. This might be a company employee, vendor, or customer. Use references *before* you meet the employer: have someone who knows the manager you want to work for call him and recommend you. Then you'll be more likely to win a date. (I call this latter approach "the proactive, preemptive reference.")

This is how I once won a job with a computer sales company. At an industry product show, I engineered a casual meeting with Gerry, a vendor who sold equipment to the company I wanted to work for. Gerry already knew me, but now he knew I was interested in working for his customer. He introduced me to Mike, an employee of my target company. Mike told me most of what I needed to know to interview intelligently with his boss. (Mike later recommended that I be hired.) In the meantime, Gerry talked with Laura, the vice president I wanted to work for, and told her what a catch I would be. Before I had an interview, the company was sold on me.

Find or create a connection. Become an insider.

6. *Find the decision maker.*

Personnel isn't going to hire you. The manager's boss isn't going to hire you. Nor will the person who screened your résumé. None of those people need you. They have no vested interest in you.

Find the guy who needs you. He's the person who has a vested interest in hiring you. If he can and wants to hire you, he will. If he doesn't, at least you got to the decision maker, and you'll have an answer. Getting to the right person won't always win you the job, but at least you'll be turned down for the right job by the right person. The wrong person will too often turn you down for any job. "The Power of Information" in chapter 6 offers suggestions about how to find the decision maker.

7. *Don't try to* **get a job.**

When you walk into a meeting with the boss, *do the job.* Don't talk about getting hired. That decision is once removed from what's important to any employer. Companies are not in the business of hiring people. They are in the business of making shoes. Be able to do what they do. Be able and ready to make a shoe for them. Become one of them. Don't make them do the hiring job. Do the shoemaking job and make their job easier. Then they'll start thinking about hiring you.

8. *Don't do an interview.*

Do a presentation. Offer a solution to a problem. Show the company how to earn more profit. Go in prepared, like a consultant, as though you will have to do all the talking. Like a consultant, a job candidate is there to solve a problem. Prove to the employer that you know that. You should know enough about the job and the company to take a good stab at convincing the employer to hire you, without the employer ever having to say a word in the interview. (What a great exercise this is, when you're planning your presentation!)

9. Turn your references into recommendations.

Don't try by yourself to convince the employer you have done good work in the past. Let the employer get independent evidence. Don't wait to be asked for references. Offer them. Better yet, don't wait for the employer to call your references. *Have your references call the person who interviewed you before he calls them.* Anyone who's going to give you an exemplary reference should be glad to make the phone call. That turns your references into *recommendations*.

10. The employer wants to hire you.

Understand one thing about the employer before you walk into an interview: he wants to hire you. (This is likely untrue of the personnel jockeys you will encounter.) He has a vested interest in your being the right candidate. If you are, he will save time, money, and anxiety, and his profits will increase when you start work.

New Interview Instructions

The *New Interview Instructions* in this chapter will help you to turn the right job interview into a job offer. If the job you are interviewing for is of interest to you, this chapter will provide you with important tools for winning an offer. Developed specifically to reflect and support the central concept of *doing the job* to win the job, these instructions will give you an edge.

By now you should have a good idea about what matters in an interview. You should understand that to an employer you represent *the power to get the job done.* When you prepare yourself to go into the interview and do the job, you exceed an employer's expectations in an unprecedented way.

Make sure you're prepared. Good jobs are hard to come by, and so are the right interviews. Don't waste the good opportunities that you've worked hard to develop.

We have talked at great length about the Four Questions and how to use your power to do the job to control an interview. While these are the keys to a job offer, there are other aspects of an interview that you should consider when doing your preparation.

Understand Your Goal

Many people make the mistake of assuming that once they have been invited to an interview, they have to decide whether or not they are ready to take the job. Nothing could be farther from the truth. You can decide whether or not you are *interested* in the job, but you can't decide whether you will accept an offer because *an offer hasn't been made to you yet.* The ball is not yet in your court. Your goal in the interview is to win an offer, to get the ball in your court. Then you can decide what to do with it.

The main purpose of this chapter is to help get the ball in your court. To give *you* the opportunity to say yes or no. Once you have the offer, then there will be *many* decisions you will have to make.

The purpose of this section is not to help you decide whether the job for which you are interviewing is suitable for you. All the instructions presume that you have done your homework, applied the Four Questions, and that you would consider the job quite seriously. Why else would you go on the interview?

I have found that when the instructions that follow are considered prior to an interview, job candidates perform better and receive offers more often. No one should memorize all the suggestions or ask all the recommended questions. Rather, you should take in the flavor of the ideas and use those suggestions that are best suited to a particular situation. If you find yourself in doubt, remember the Four Questions:

- Do I understand the job that needs to be done?
- Am I demonstrating to the employer that I can do the job?
- Am I showing I can do the job the way the employer wants it done?
- Have I convinced the employer I can do the job profitably for his company?

If you or the interviewer are stumbling during an interview, raise and answer one or more of the Four Questions. It will put you back on track, and back in control.

First Impressions

When you meet the interviewer, be cordial. It is surprising how often a job candidate forgets this when he has other things on his mind, especially if he is a little nervous. If you are cordial, you will not only break the ice but also relax. You will bring your "scared self" under control.

You're more than a job candidate waiting to be questioned: you are a thoughtful, prepared expert meeting someone new who needs your help. Be sociable. Don't be too "professionally stiff." Use a confident, friendly tone of voice. Relax. Talk. Ask questions. Discuss. Explore. The interviewer's first impression of you will affect the entire interview.

Attire and Grooming

The rule of thumb is to dress well. *Your attire should reflect the standards of the industry and the job you are seeking.* If you usually dress very casually for work, dress more formally for your interview. Men should always wear a tie to an interview, and at least a sport coat if not a suit. Women should wear their most professional business attire. Both men and women should avoid splashy colors, unnecessary jewelry, and heavy aftershave or perfume. Shoes must be polished. Your clothes should be neatly pressed, not wrinkled. The interviewer expects that you will be trying to make a good impression, so don't worry about being a little overdressed. As long as you look professional, you're safe.

Good grooming is very important. Hair should be combed, or fixed in a style appropriate to the job you're seeking. Trim your nails. (I can't believe how many men I meet whose fingernails have not been neatly trimmed.) If you don't normally use a good deodorant, use one before the interview and plan to use it all the time. The same goes for mouthwash. When someone doesn't know you, it's the little things they notice first and remember longest, so attend to them.

You will find a lot of very specific advice in some books about color, style, and other attire and grooming issues. Bear in mind that tastes vary, sometimes very significantly across industries and geographic regions. There is no way to tell what a particular person might think of what you're wearing. If you go too far in following someone's advice about what's "best," you may encounter an interviewer who disagrees. You could end up shooting yourself in the foot.

The solution to this problem is to look like *yourself,* and to be your most *presentable* self. Put your best foot forward. If you really doubt your judgment, find a good, conservative clothing shop and get advice about how to dress professionally. Don't let anyone turn you into someone you don't recognize in the mirror.

The Four Questions: The Keys to the Job

An interviewer wants to know many things about you, and he has only a short time to learn what he needs to know. There are four key things he wants to know more than anything else. If you can respond positively to these four questions, the ground will be set for an offer:

1. Do you understand the job that needs to be done?
2. Can you do the job?

3. Can you do the job the way the employer wants it done?
4. Can you do the job profitably for the company?

No matter what the employer asks during an interview, the Four Questions are what he needs answers to. Without answers to these questions, an employer cannot make a responsible decision about hiring you. If he doesn't ask you these questions directly, then ask them for him and make sure you provide the answers. If you have to, state clearly,

1. "As I understand it, the work you need to have done is:

_____

_____."

2. "Here is why I can do this work and how I would do it:

_____

_____."

3. "It seems important to you that the job be done this way:

_____

_____."

4. "I can make this job more profitable to your company by:

_____

_____."

Having covered the Four Questions in chapter 2, I won't go into more detail here except to point out that they represent the foundation of every successful interview. I can't emphasize enough the importance of your communicating to the employer the answers to these questions. If he doesn't ask for this information and you don't provide it, you will experience one of several undesirable outcomes.

- You will not win an offer, because the manager doesn't know whether you can do the job.
- You will be put on a list of *maybes*—candidates the employer is not sure about—and you will wait while he interviews dozens of other candidates.
- He may hire you anyway, but you will wind up working for a manager who blames you for not doing the work the way he wants it done.

The Fine Points

While this foundation is being laid during an interview, the employer will be covering some finer points with you. Through my years of headhunting experience, acquired while working with major corporations as well as smaller businesses, I have learned that these are the other questions an employer is asking about you:

1. Can you get along with him?
2. Do you communicate effectively?
3. Are you interested in the work?
4. Are you motivated and enthusiastic? Are you ready to tackle your work each day without much supervision?
5. Do you have the technical expertise he needs?
6. Can you make a significant contribution to his group?
7. Do you want the job?

You should think about each of these questions before you go on a particular interview. Don't get wrapped up in how to answer these questions, because all the answers are simple: yes. Together, these yeses represent your attitude about your work. Attitude is best communicated by your behavior. The key, as with the Four Questions, is to *demonstrate* the answers.

The advice that follows will help to complete your understanding about what makes an interview a success, for you and for an employer. It will give you some ideas about how to demonstrate your positive attitude about your work.

1. Demonstrate that you can get along with the manager.

When the interview turns to questions about your interests, past jobs, hobbies, and so on, the interviewer is trying to get a feel for your personality. He wants to know if you can get along with him and whether he would enjoy working with you. He needs to decide whether he likes you.

Talk about yourself when the employer asks you to, but don't go on and on about yourself. It's important to let the interviewer know you are interested in him as well. It's a show of respect and a demonstration of your interest in forming a good relationship.

People love to talk about themselves, to share their attitudes and experiences with others. Doing this forms a subtle bond between people. Promote this bond during your meeting. Turn the discussion around to the interviewer. Show an interest in who he is, but don't be presumptuous or ask personal questions. A good compromise is to give him an opportunity to tell you about himself in the context of his work. You can ask the interviewer:

- What led you to work in this industry?
- What other kinds of work have you done?
- What do you find most exciting about your current project?
- What concerns do you have about it?

You don't have to ask these specific questions. You can come up with similar ones of your own. Ask them in the course of conversation; there is no need to press for answers. Remember, you are trying to establish a comfortable relationship with the interviewer. You want to show you are interested in him and can get along with him. (You might have guessed that the last question above is a great lead-in to showing the manager how you can tackle a live problem.)

2. Be a good communicator.

The interviewer wants to learn about you. The more he learns, the more he will feel he has invested his time well in your meeting. Help him out.

The interviewer has a large degree of control in the interview, but it is up to you to help him learn what he needs to know about you. To do this, you must be sure you are communicating effectively. You should let him lead the discussion, but you should also offer useful information on your own.

Sometimes, employers feel that talking with job candidates is like "pulling teeth." A lot of candidates just sit and wait for the next question. They answer it and wait for another. They don't volunteer much information. They act like cows (see chapter 5). Employers hate that. It suggests to them that if the candidate is hired, he will probably need a lot of direction and supervision.

Employers want to hire self-motivated people who can engage in a meaningful discussion. People who can think on their feet and contribute good ideas without being asked; people who can work well on their own.

> Being a good communicator means answering questions appropriately. It also means *asking* appropriate questions, *offering* your ideas without always being asked, and *showing* what you can do.

The more communicative you are in your interview, the more competent the manager will perceive you to be.* If he has to pull teeth to get information from you, he will quickly develop the impression that you are difficult to work with.

It's important to keep in mind that you are not expected to know

---

* Of course, this doesn't mean that you should ramble and monopolize the conversation. Ask some friends or coworkers for their opinions. It's always better to hear criticism from a friend.

everything. In fact, most managers consider it an important skill to *recognize when you don't understand something* and to *know when to ask for clarification or help.* So don't feel that every question you are asked is a do-or-die challenge. Sometimes the best answer is another question. Ask the manager to clarify anything that's not clear to you.

Turn each of your answers into a discussion. Create a conversation. Work *with* the employer. In your answers, give examples from your own experience. Ask the interviewer for examples from his experience.

A final point on this topic: try to read the interviewer's mind, just a little. We all do this in everyday conversation. It's an important aspect of human communication, and it's absolutely crucial both in an interview and on the job. It's the main reason for all the research I encourage you to do. Unfortunately, the traditional rules about interviewing have programmed people to think they should wait for the manager to ask questions before they speak. That is, people wait for the manager to *tell* them what's on his mind. In fact, you should use what you know to *guess* what the employer is thinking. Your prospective boss wants to know that at least some of the time, you can guess what he wants without his saying so. It's part of being able to work together.

You have done a lot of research on this company's business. Put it to good use. Try to understand what is most important to the interviewer, and then try to focus on and discuss these topics in depth. As long as you are being honest, it is important to tell the interviewer what he wants to hear on the topics he wants to discuss.

3. Demonstrate your interest in the work and the company.

During your meeting, the employer will discuss his company and the project he is working on. Obviously, you have to show you have the skills to do the work. That's what doing the job is all about.

It is equally important for you to indicate that you *find the work interesting.* Even if you demonstrate the right technical skills, the manager will not hire you unless you also show that you are interested in the work. Here are a few things you can ask to indicate your interest:

- What is the importance of this project to the company?
- What do you find most challenging about it?
- What kinds of difficulties have you had with this project?
- How could this project be made into a big success?
- In what directions would you like to see your department go?
- What qualities are most important to you in the people who work for you?

Notice that most of these questions indicate your interest *in the work you would be doing, and in the work the manager does.* These are the kinds of things a concerned employee discusses with his manager. Act like an employee. You don't want to grill the manager, but it is important to let him know that you are interested in more than just answering his questions: you are interested in him, in the job, and in the success of his team.

4. Display your motivation and enthusiasm.

Aside from your skills and expertise, perhaps the most important qualities you can possess are motivation and enthusiasm. These are different from your interest in the work. You might be interested in the building of a space shuttle, but you might not be very motivated or enthusiastic about doing that work yourself.

Motivation is a desire that is powerful enough to make you act. *Enthusiasm* is excitement, an eagerness to involve yourself with whatever you're working on.

To a manager, it doesn't matter what you know or what you can do if you aren't enthusiastic about doing it and motivated to do it well. The best employee is the one who wants to take the ball and run with it.

In the interview, the manager is trying to determine whether you will pick up the ball and how far you are willing to run with it on your own. He needs to know whether he will have to spend a lot of his valuable time supervising (or "micromanaging") you, or whether you will "go" on your own.

Now, this is not to say that a manager expects you'll never turn to him for help. What I mean is that he expects you'll know when to ask for help and when to solve a problem independently. If you are a motivated individual and you can function well on your own, you will be a strong asset—even a leader—to the team.

In an interview, you can demonstrate your motivation and enthusiasm in many ways:

- Ask to see how the company's products are created.
- If it is a services company, ask what makes its services special.
- Tell about things you've done that prove you are self-motivated:

  Projects where you went "the extra mile"
  New ideas you had that benefited your past employers
  Awards or recognition you received for doing a good job

- Volunteer one or two ideas that might improve *this* company's product or service. Explain how you would implement your ideas.
- Discuss your possible contributions to the employer's project.
- Ask whether there is a special task force or project team on which you could serve. Go the extra mile.
- Suggest to the manager that he let you show him how you would do the job. Offer to work for him for an hour or two.
- Explain why doing this kind of work is important to you.

Motivation is a personal thing that cannot be easily faked. It makes a person stand out. The Four Questions will help you verify the true level of your own motivation about a particular job. As you start doing all the work necessary to answer them, you'll know whether or not you're really motivated to win that job.

Think of other ways you can communicate your enthusiasm for your work to an employer. The ideas above will get you started. Remember, motivation is desire turned into action. Don't just talk, *act.* The most powerful demonstration of enthusiasm is to *tell the employer you want the job.* When you *do the job* in the interview, you reveal the power of your motivation.

5. Demonstrate your technical expertise.

A good interviewer will ask specific technical questions as well as broad "tell all you know" questions. He may also present some scenarios and ask how you would deal with them. Don't just respond to his questions: *do the job* during the interview.

Apply what you know. Solve the employer's specific problems. Suggest how you would use your knowledge and abilities to do the job for which you are interviewing. For example, if the manager asks you what you think is a good way to handle a difficult customer, tell him. Then ask him what kinds of difficult customers he encounters in his work. Explain how you would use your skills to handle *those specific customers.* Go the extra step. Show concern for his *specific problems.* (More suggestions about how to demonstrate your technical expertise are presented in "Do the Job During the Interview" in chapter 4.)

6. Make a contribution.

To distinguish yourself from the cows, you must engage in a discussion in a *problem-solving* context. Contribute something useful. People are often hired because in their interviews they solve a problem with which the manager has been grappling. So approach the company *as though you were already working there* and being paid to use your knowledge. Act like a good consultant. Act like a good employee.

7. Make it clear that you want the job.

All too often, a candidate for a job leaves the interview convinced he did well. He wants the job and thinks the interviewer knows it. But he has not explicitly expressed his interest. This can be a fatal mistake.

> The interviewer knows you want the job *only if you tell him you want the job.*

It doesn't matter what comments you successfully "slipped into the conversation" to make him think you want the job. *You have to tell him.* My wife would never have married me if I hadn't come out and explicitly told her I loved her. Similarly, I would never hire someone who didn't specifically come out and tell me he wanted to work with me. *People need to hear a commitment.*

Make the commitment.

Keep in mind that until a company makes you an offer, the ball is not in your court. You have no real decision to make until an offer is presented to you. Completing an interview without letting the interviewer know you want an offer is like playing basketball without ever trying to make a basket. You can't just dribble and pass. You have to shoot.

> If you would consider an offer from the company, *you must take action.*

The employer doesn't expect you'll accept an offer on the spot. But he would like to know how motivated you are to do the work. Most interviewers will never ask you. *They want you to take the initiative and tell them.*

Make a commitment at the end of the interview. If you want the job (assuming the offer is right), say so:

"I want this job. I hope I have convinced you that I can do it, and do it well. I would enjoy working on your team. I would seriously consider an offer from you." Look the manager directly in the eye and *maintain eye contact* as you say this.

Remember, this doesn't mean that you have to accept an offer if he makes it. The offer must be as attractive as the job. This is a crucial distinction. The commitment you have made is to *the work and the job*, not to any particular salary or other employment terms. Everything else still needs to be discussed. It is perfectly legitimate to turn down an offer for a job you really want, if the offer isn't acceptable and you can't negotiate a mutually acceptable deal (see "The Power of the Offer" in chapter 6).

If the employer doesn't make you an offer, you have no choice to make at all. So, if you're interested, say so, and say it clearly. *Win that offer.*

Get a Commitment from the Employer

Part of being the right person for a job is *wanting the job*. Why should an employer offer the job to someone who doesn't want it? It's up to you to make that commitment. But it is also up to you to win a commitment from the employer.

At the end of an interview you have the manager's attention, and he's giving it willingly. Use the opportunity to your best advantage. *Obtain a commitment* from the employer. This is *the only way* to avoid that most frustrating aspect of job hunting: waiting for the company to call you back and tell you whether they're interested in you.

You shared some of your valuable time, and you made a commitment. You deserve to know what the manager thinks of you. Ask:

- Do you think I would fit into your team?
- Are you as interested in me as I am in working for you?
- I'd like to meet the other members of your team. Would that be possible?
- Can you give me a tour of your facility?

A positive response from the manager to any of these questions is not a guarantee that you will receive an offer, but it constitutes a commitment. Help him make it. If he does, he has opened the door to further discussion about actually hiring you. Take advantage of it!

The Truth About Employment Tests

Technical Tests

If you are asked to take a technical or "skills" test, don't feel insulted. Some interviewers use tests as a quick, effective way to survey your skills. Bear in mind that the personnel jockeys have sent a lot of candidates to this manager for his evaluation. He's using the test to help him make an initial cut, or to help him identify topics to discuss with you. Again, you are not expected to know everything. You are expected to be creative and do your best.

After a test the interviewer will take the time to probe more deeply into your skills and to discuss larger issues. If you have questions regarding the test, ask them. Some tests can actually help you learn more about the job.

The best technical tests (especially oral ones) are not designed to determine which mathematical equations or technical facts (be they physical laws, financial rules, or machine settings) you can remember. Numbers, tables, and rules can be found in handbooks. Problem-solving ability is what an employer is paying for when he hires you. Consequently, an interviewer is usually more concerned about *how you think*.

Your aim should be to think clearly and to reveal your problem-solving strategies. Your answer might turn out wrong, but your strategy is usually what counts. So, be sure to describe *how* you are solving a problem, and what you would do if you needed special information to solve it. If you can't remember a formula, say so, then go on to explain where you would find the formula, and how you would use it to solve the problem.

Psychological Tests

Psychological tests are a different story. Under certain circumstances, they can contradict one of the main ideas in this book: *You should always control how you are represented to an employer.* This means you should take care that someone else (or something) does not misrepresent you. This includes personnel jockeys and psychological tests.

Make sure the hiring manager gets the accurate story about you, and make sure you know what that "story" is. A test can potentially convey inaccurate information about you. It can also convey information that you are unaware of, if you are not privy to the results of your test.

Some psychological tests are completely legitimate. Some, to be blunt, are downright sneaky. A legitimate test can be used in a sneaky way by an unscrupulous interviewer. In the worst case, a good test can be administered and interpreted by an unskilled person to draw the wrong conclusions about you.

If you have never taken a psychological test, I recommend taking two or three different ones just for the experience. You will learn some interesting things. However, it's not advisable to take your first test under the pressure of an interview situation. Call the psychology or sociology department of a local college and ask them to recommend a testing organization, or ask if they can administer one to you.

There are all sorts of psychological tests. The most common ones are called *personality* or *interest inventories.* These tests compare your attitudes and interests to those of thousands of other people in specific occupations. The intent is to determine how similar your attitudes or interests are to those of the typical person in a certain occupation. Usually, the results of these tests are used by a company to confirm their own impressions of you.

As you might suspect, a test that compares your attitudes and interests to what is considered "average" or "typical" may not portray you accurately. Make an informed decision about how to handle such tests if you're asked to take one. Learn how you perform on psychological tests by taking one or two privately. If you decide to let an employer administer a psychological test, it is reasonable to ask that the results and interpretation be shared with you. You might also ask about the credentials of the person who scored and analyzed the test you took. If you are going to be judged by a test whose results will be unknown to you, you are putting yourself at a disadvantage.

If you refuse to take a test, don't climb on a soapbox and complain about tests. Politely decline to take the test and explain that you understand your decision may rule you out as a candidate. Be prepared to lose the interview at this point, but don't blame the interviewer. Like it or not, you are in his house, playing by his rules. If you don't share his attitude about tests, it is better to find out now and part company on good terms.

If you choose to end an interview because you don't like what you see or hear, or because you are asked to do something you would rather not do, always leave politely.

Your attitude about tests (or about anything else that turns into a deal breaker) does not make you right and the interviewer wrong. Be man or woman enough to disagree without being rude, and without insisting you are right. You may run into this person again. It's not worth leaving a bad impression behind, no matter how right you are. It could cost you dearly at a later date.

Working for a Job vs. Working for Free

Doing a job to win a job does not mean that you should agree to work for free, so that the employer can "try you out." I do not believe that anyone should work for free. A person's skills are valuable, and value should always be exchanged for equal value.

A few years ago a respected professional journal brought to light the fact that a handful of unscrupulous employers were assigning take-home tasks to job candidates to get some free work out of them without any intention of paying or hiring them. Such a practice is reprehensible. Never give away your work. Don't ever confuse *doing the job* with being taken advantage of by an employer.

However, for every example of unsavory employment practices, there are a dozen examples of people with integrity who are willing to trust one another enough to try to jump-start new work relationships. This just proves that employers and job hunters are capable—and willing—to break the traditional rules of interviewing so that they can get the job done.

I once worked with a fine engineer named Sam who wanted more than anything in the world to work for a certain computer company. The manager liked Sam but wasn't sure he could really do the job. Sam was from another part of the world and his English was not yet good enough to enable him to always communicate effectively. But his enthusiasm and motivation came through clearly.

After consulting with me, Sam suggested to the manager that the company let him do the job for a week with no pay, so that Sam could demonstrate conclusively the value he would bring to the company. If they didn't like his performance, Sam would leave without any hard feelings. I offered to put my money where my mouth was by not billing the company for my fee unless Sam was hired permanently. The manager was a bit startled, but he agreed to stifle the objections of his personnel department so that this ambitious fellow could put an unusual spin on *doing the job to win the job.*

Before the trial week was up, the manager called to tell me he was going to not only hire Sam but also pay him for the three days he'd already worked. Sam went on to become a successful manager himself.

Did this work out because Sam was such a good engineer? Or, was the manager influenced by the fact that Sam was willing to prove himself first? I think the answer is, some of both. The manager was impressed with Sam's confidence, his enthusiasm, and his motivation, and—perhaps most important—Sam's belief that his ability to *do the job* would win him the job. Sam put action ahead of talk, and he put doing the work ahead of getting the job. All of these things revealed Sam's powerful work ethic to his new boss.

This experience involved an employer who possessed an extraordinary degree of integrity. It is a valuable story because it proves a point I tried to make early in this book. *Left to their own devices, and ignoring all the traditional rules about interviewing, a good worker and a good manager will find ways to create a good working relationship.*

I do not provide this illustration of my point to encourage you to attempt a similar approach. You must judge what is legitimate in a particular situation and decide what is right for you. Likewise, if a prospective employer makes an unusual request to see how you perform, you have to judge for yourself what is reasonable and what is not.

Remember that the best way to win a job is to show the prospective employer that you can do the job he needs to have done. That is the entire purpose of an interview, and that's how you should use your interview time.

The Big Secret

Over the years, I have worked with large and small businesses, helping them to define their job requirements, meet the right people, and hire the best workers. I carefully advised every job candidate I sent on an interview, and I talked with the employers and the candidates after their meetings. I have learned a lot from all of these people. In this book I've tried to share the greatest piece of wisdom that I've garnered from my experience.

Job candidates ask me one question over and over again: *What is the secret to winning the job?*

Doing a job is the best way to win the job.

I'm sorry it's such a secret. I wish everyone knew it.

Although I have spent most of my life running my own business, I have also worked for a few companies. I used this secret to win every one of those jobs. As a manager, I used it to evaluate workers I interviewed. As a headhunter, I used it to help job candidates win jobs—the *right* candidates and the *right* jobs.

How can you do a job before you're hired? Act like you have the job. *Don't treat the interview as an interview.* Go to the interview as though it's your first day on the job.

When you go after any job, apply the Four Questions:

- First, make sure you understand it.
- Second, demonstrate that you can do it.
- Third, show that you can do it the way the employer wants it done.
- Finally, prove that you can do it profitably for the employer and for you.

If you accomplish this, you will find you are pursuing the *right* job and interviewing with the power that wins job offers.

Summary

Here is a brief review of the most important attributes that you as a job candidate need to demonstrate and communicate in an interview before an employer will extend an offer to you. I have changed the order of the points made earlier because I want to demonstrate the flexibility of the Four Questions in preparing you for the interview. At the same time, I want to emphasize that you should not memorize these concepts in any particular way. What matters is that you understand them and be able to apply them when you think and talk about your work. You must clearly convey to the employer that:

1. *You understand the work he needs to have done. If the employer is not convinced you understand the work to be done, you will not be hired.*

   If you don't understand it, you must ask more questions until you do. Then you must repeat it back, so that the employer is satisfied you understand it.

2. *You can do the job. That is, you possess the skills necessary to do the work the way the employer wants the work to be done.*

   Ask the employer whether you have demonstrated this to his satisfaction. If not, ask him what you failed to demonstrate, and then demonstrate it. If it turns out you really can't do the job the way the employer wants it done, read chapter 9.

3. *You can do the job profitably for the company.*

   If you don't see the connection between this job and the company's profitability, ask the interviewer for help. How does he think the job you've applied for could be done more profitably? How does the job fit into his long-term profitability goals? The best approach is to think these questions through for yourself before you go to the interview. Consider issues that affect the company and explore how they might affect the company's profitability. It is important to understand how the job you're interviewing for fits into that analysis.

4. *You are motivated to do the work, and you are enthusiastic about doing it.*

5. *You are interested in the work and the people on the team.*

   One of the very important requests you can make, at a comfortable time during your interview, is to meet other members of the manager's team. You can also ask what other departments the position would have to interact with and request to meet the managers of those teams. Don't overdo this, but try to meet at least a couple of your future coworkers.

6. *You can work well with the manager.*

You listen well and you understand; you are capable of anticipating some of the group's technical problems; you can effectively communicate your suggestions in a useful form; and you can work well in a group environment.

7. *You can make a significant contribution to the company.*

Your contribution can take the form of high-quality work that indirectly reduces costs, or it might directly improve the company's bottom line. Your work might also contribute to other aspects of success, such as the development of new products or the creation of new ways of doing business. What constitutes a significant contribution will depend on the company and on the nature of the work. Just remember: there's a big difference between agreeing to show up for work each day and *enlisting* in the effort to make the company more successful.

8. *You want the job.*

I can't tell you how many times I have seen a company jump over a highly qualified candidate and hire one who was a little less qualified but who *clearly wanted the job* and *clearly wanted to work on the manager's team.*

This is not a "wish list." You already possess these attributes in one form or another; however, just having them isn't enough. You must thoughtfully approach the interview intending to communicate these attributes to the interviewer.

Don't Be Overwhelmed

Don't let all of this information overwhelm you. Neither you nor the interviewer will do everything right in the interview—and that's okay. If you make sure you cover the job itself in your interview by applying the concepts we have discussed, you will create an interview atmosphere unlike any the manager has ever encountered. You will have created *The New Interview.* You will stand out as an unusual candidate whose goal is to help the manager solve a problem and get a job done.

If you are anxious about your meeting with your prospective employer, you can lessen your anxiety by giving yourself more control and confidence. Sit down with a few sheets of clean paper and a pen. Go through this book and mark the topics you are most concerned about, or which you think are most important to helping you achieve your goals. Review the suggestions I have made and write down how you would use each suggestion. Be specific. Write down the things you want to say to the interviewer. Write down your questions. Write down important points you want to convey to him. Write down *the things you are going to do* in the interview.

An approach that I find works well is to write down *advice you would offer to a good friend,* as if he were going on the interview instead of you. This will allow you to step back and be a little more objective.

You still won't remember everything in the book, or everything you wrote down. However, research and experience show that if you force yourself to think something through and then write it down, you will remember it better and you will be able to *integrate it* into your presentation. This will help—I guarantee it. The investment of your time will pay off handsomely.

CHAPTER 8

Master Your "Self"

The Fun Facts of Behavior Change

Having a background in cognitive psychology does not necessarily make someone a better businessperson. However, I have found over the years that there are quite a few concepts I learned in the world of psychology that I have always—often without being aware of it—applied in my work. These concepts are not mysterious; it's just that most people outside of the research community aren't exposed to them. I've often felt I had a business advantage because I understood them.

My good friend and former research partner Dr. Stephen A. Small, who is an expert in the field of human behavior, refers to the ideas I'm going to review below as some of "the fun facts of psychology." These concepts *are* fun because they're so practical and because when you think about them, they seem so *obvious*. More important, they subtly determine the outcome of so many of our daily activities. I'd like to share some of these concepts with you here, with the intention of stimulating some positive changes in the way you think and act with regard to interviews. Change can be a difficult thing; the first step can seem impossibly high. A new idea might seem simple enough, but actually putting it into practice can be a little intimidating, or even terrifying. This is where you can use the "fun facts of psychology" to your benefit.

You cannot accomplish the goals set out in this book unless you take some bold steps before, during, and after your interviews. If you have never attempted to control an interview, you may wonder how you're going to get up the gumption to try. We all sweat a little when trying new things, and it usually takes a few tries to get them right. But that's true of most people. Perhaps the most important thing I've learned in studying the psychology of behavior change is that *it can be done.*

Because change is a central requirement for success in your job hunt, we will briefly review some relevant findings from the world of psychological research. Therefore, this chapter is about the factors that affect our ability to control the way we act, and our ability to act successfully.

It is beyond the scope of this book to discuss specific instructions about how to *implement* behavior change. If you want to read more, you might want to pick up a psychology text at a college book store (see "Recommended Reading" on page 211). I use the same terminology that psychology researchers use, so you will be able to easily follow up on whatever concepts interest you the most.

None of what follows is magical or mysterious. A lot of research is done every year on how people think, behave, and change. The pity is, few people hear much about it because researchers have a terrible habit of sharing their knowledge only with one another in obscure academic journals. Once you have access to some of their findings, it's not very difficult to apply this new knowledge to your own life.

Mastering Self-Fulfilling Prophecy

Are you scared? Afraid you will fail? Then you will—unless you carefully program yourself *to be in control* and *to succeed.*

The research on self-fulfilling prophecy suggests that people predict their own future, and then they wind up making it happen—or fulfilling it—in much the way they predicted. Successful people predict success; unsuccessful people predict failure.* Here's an example of how negative thoughts can adversely affect your behavior. If you are playing basketball and you think that you are going to miss a basket, you will get so tense that you will twitch or lose fine control of your shooting arm, thereby increasing the chance that you will miss the basket. By predicting failure, you affected your behavior, which in turn influenced the outcome of your efforts. In much the same way, if you think you are going to be nervous in an interview, you will *make yourself nervous* and that will cause problems.

This kind of anxious, insecure thinking is like a personal prediction, or prophecy, that we make come true, as though we want to prove we were right. Once a person starts on this vicious cycle of predicting-then-causing failure for himself, the consequences can be debilitating. The negative attitude begins to feed on the negative experiences it has caused. Job search and interviewing are perfect examples of highly stressful activities where one or two failures can quickly destroy confidence, leaving a person feeling as though he has forgotten how to "do it right." A person first fears, and then begins to expect, more failure. Through his negative attitude, he ends up unconsciously sabotaging his own efforts. The good news is that change is possible. It just takes a little time and practice.

Here's how it works. Don't try to change your negative attitude. Because attitudes and thoughts are difficult to pinpoint, they are difficult to change. So, if you have a negative attitude, ignore it for a little while. Instead, focus on something you can see and change more easily: the behavior associated with it. What makes this approach work so well is that you change just one small aspect of your behavior at a time, until you conquer the whole thing.

Act the way you wish you could be acting—the way you know is right. Even if your "scared self" is predicting failure, *perform the behavior you know is right anyway.* Take it a step at a time—you don't need to change your behavior all at once.

---

*I am generalizing a bit here for the sake of clarity. For a more detailed discussion of self-fulfilling prophecy, check a good introductory psychology text.

Try to exert a new level of control over a small part of your behavior. When you do positive things, soon you will see some positive effects, whether you "predict" them or not. Sooner or later you will begin to see that your "forced" behavior is producing positive results, even if they are only small ones. Then take the next step, the next positive action, no matter how small, no matter how imperfect. Do it the best way you know how. But do it.

The small positive experiences you have will begin to generate little feelings of success. These will encourage you to do more. The little successes will become bigger successes. And why not? You're doing what you set out to do! You will start to believe more in yourself. You will start to trust yourself. Your successful behavior will lead you to start *predicting success* for yourself. This new attitude will in turn produce behavior that results in more success.

The most important thing to remember is that you don't have to do it all at once; *you must do it step by step.*

Chapter 6 is all about changing your prophecies about interviews by changing your interview preparation behavior. The employment industry has taught us that finding a job is an inflexible, regimented process over which we have little control. This is simply not true, unless a person makes it true by going on the wrong interviews, being ill prepared, and contracting interview-itis.

To change your prophecy about interviewing, change your behavior. Start gathering the information discussed in chapter 6. This is effective behavior. It will make you smarter. It will help you make better choices. Your new knowledge will make you more confident. You will feel in control because you will be in control. This will reduce your fear and anxiety about interviews. Consequently, you will interview more effectively and more successfully.

Overcoming Learned Helplessness

When the employment system encourages you to "play the numbers" by mailing out lots of résumés to lots of employers, it's setting you up for rejection after rejection—and none of the rejection seems to be due to any failure of your own. How *could* it be? All you did was stick a piece of paper in the mail! Nonetheless, the rejections come, and they lead to a sense of helplessness. How could so many companies *not want you?* If so many companies have said *no!* to you, how are you going to get anyone to say yes? It all seems so hopeless.

Let's take a look at what's really happening to the millions of discouraged job hunters around America—and how you can avoid becoming one of them. I'm going to tell you about some research that will make animal lovers quake, and rightfully so. However, I'm going to tell you about it because there is an important message in it.

Researchers put a white rat in a rather unusual cage. The floor of the cage was electrified, so that the researcher could give the rat a mild shock by pressing a button. The cage also had a little "safe room" off to the side that was not electrified. When the researcher pressed the shock button, a buzzer would sound first, warning the rat that a shock was coming in a few seconds. Then the shock came. After a few shocks, the rat learned that when the buzzer sounded it was a good idea to run into the safe room. Whenever the researcher tried to shock the rat, the rat usually took the warning and escaped to safety.

In a separate setup, the researchers put a second rat in an electrified cage without a safe room. This rat also heard a warning buzzer before the shock, but he had nowhere to run. The buzzer would sound and the rat would scamper around the cage, trying to escape the shock. Soon, the rat learned he could not escape, so he would helplessly sit in the corner and wait to be shocked. He had *learned* to behave helplessly, because there was no escape.

Then the researchers did something interesting. They put the second rat in the cage that had the safe room (the rat was "shown" the safe room). No matter how many times they sounded the buzzer, the rat sat on the electrified section of floor and accepted the shock. The rat had learned to be helpless. It had given up trying to escape a painful experience, even when it could.

Job hunters read want ads and send out résumés. They get no responses. They go on some interviews, and then wait for weeks or months for a decision. Nothing happens. They get no job offers. So they send out more résumés. People are turned down for jobs, with little or no explanation. They keep at it, never knowing when or where they will get a job offer. The employment industry wears them down, and after a while, job hunters come to expect that this is just the way it is.

Like the second rat, job hunters learn to be helpless, because in their experience there is little correlation between their traditional job hunting efforts and whether they win a job. So, they become one of the millions who helplessly repeat unprofitable behavior, hoping a kind personnel jockey will call them with a job offer.

> One of the purposes of this book is to help you to avoid this sense of helplessness, and to show how you can control what happens to you in the course of seeking a job.

Create a New Attitude by Changing Your Behavior

Helplessness, like fear or anxiety, is a learned attitude. After experiencing failure many times, a person gives up. It doesn't matter that the world around him has changed to make success possible. Like the helpless rat, the job hunter gives up and never changes his behavior.

The only way you can change a hopeless or negative attitude about interviewing is to *act differently*. Research has shown that people do not change their attitudes just by thinking about them.

They change their attitudes by *first changing their behavior*. And that's what this book is all about!

Research done in the past fifteen years on the control of phobias (irrational fears) centers on this relationship between attitudes and behavior. One set of particularly interesting studies involves snake phobics (people who are extremely afraid of snakes). A psychologist uses *behavior control* techniques to change a snake phobic's negative attitude, or fear, of snakes.

A snake phobic's fear is gradually eliminated by helping him to progressively think about, look at, touch, and finally play with harmless snakes. Positive experiences with snakes help to eliminate the person's fear, and that in turn alters his attitude. After playing with a harmless snake a person is forced to realize that if he is able to actually hold a snake, he must not be so afraid of snakes. Repeated experience holding snakes produces a positive change in attitude.

Sure, you say. A person who is deathly afraid of snakes is going to willingly hold a snake in his or her hands. Right.

You might think I'm also going to claim that if you are deathly afraid of interviews, you are going to change your attitude by going on interviews! What I am claiming is that if you modify your interview preparation behavior *to make it more effective and rewarding*, your attitude will follow. Let's look at how and why this works.

Behavior Change Through Successive Approximation

For snake phobics, the ultimate goal is to be able to hold a snake without experiencing fear. The psychologist takes the phobic down the path to this goal, little step by little step. Psychologists refer to this process of step-by-step change as *successive approximation* toward the desired behavior.

The little steps are each designed to be easy, and they arouse no more anxiety than the patient can reasonably deal with. The phobic is gradually exposed to snakes, first through written stories about them, and later through pictures and films. The phobic then observes a live snake through a thick glass window. With each experience, the phobic begins to feel more in control. He experiences success in controlling his fear and feels good about it. This success, however small, encourages him to continue.

Later, the phobic stands in the same room while the psychologist holds and plays with a snake. Finally, the patient touches, strokes, then holds the snake himself. By working step-by-step in this way, the "cure rate" for snake phobics is phenomenal.*

You might have noticed that part of what the snake phobic is doing is *practicing* behaviors that pay off for him. As another example, consider the various programs around the United States that help people eliminate negative attitudes about public speaking by practicing behavior-change techniques. In one of these programs, Toastmasters International, a group of people meet to help one another eliminate their anxiety about public speaking. They do it by repeatedly getting up in front of the group to make presentations on various topics. The topics don't matter. However, a participant must *prepare* his presentation; he can't just talk off the top of his head. After doing several presentations, the participants lose their anxiety because they have experienced more and more success. Consequently, their public speaking abilities improve.

These people know there's really nothing to be afraid of, but thinking about it logically doesn't change their attitudes. The programs they participate in help to eliminate their negative attitude by helping them to *change their behavior* first. Practice makes perfect. Practice also makes confidence and control.

---

* Some of the most interesting research on overcoming snake phobia has been done by Dr. Albert Bandura of Stanford University, one of the most widely cited behavior researchers in the world. Bandura's *Social Learning Theory*, listed in "Recommended Readings," provides a basic discussion of his work on self-efficacy, which is both simple and profound.

What does this mean for you? The employment industry has instilled negative attitudes and a form of helplessness in job hunters. In order to change these attitudes, and to change the way you act in regard to job hunting, you must be able to change the component actions that make up the big one. By changing each of these behavior components *successively,* or one at a time, you will build up the confidence and skill you need to *approximate* the new behavior you want to achieve. With practice, you will achieve better performance.

Let's look at an example. If you're skeptical about the idea that doing a lot of in-depth research is going to help you to find the right job, I don't really expect you to change your attitude (which would in turn lead you to change your entire job hunting strategy). I could argue with you, but that would be fruitless. In a sense, you believe what you've been taught by the employment system. Your attitude is probably based on a whole collection of experiences you've had, and there's no way to reject them with any confidence.

However, I can suggest that instead of adopting my way of thinking, you read just one issue of *Forbes* magazine and identify *one company* that seems like it would be a great place to work. That's a start. It's not complicated, and it's a behavior that you can easily perform. If you then follow up and make one phone call—to a person mentioned in the article—to gather some specific information about that company, I'll bet you'll like the outcome, and you'll be motivated to do it again. The success of those two simple behaviors—reading a magazine and calling one person on the phone—will likely make you believe that gathering specific information can lead to more fruitful discussions with employers.

By changing a couple of your behaviors, I've begun to change your attitude about job search. Why? Because I've helped you put a couple of successes under your belt. Small ones, but successes nonetheless. Now you're more likely to take courage and have confidence that you can perform those behaviors again with another company. You will also comfortably graduate to other new behaviors and attitudes as a result of these first few changes. More important, your positive new attitude will motivate you to continue.

That's how change starts, and that's how you start prophesying and enjoying *positive outcomes.*

I wrote this book to help illuminate and change the ineffective attitudes and traditions that produce failure in the job hunt. I also wrote it to show you what specific behaviors you need to practice if you are to take control of your job hunt and find the job that's right for you.

Always keep in mind that the Four Questions are the best place to start, because they will guide you toward appropriate behavior. Ask the questions about a particular job; don't worry about the interview. Then do some research. Take the small steps first. Do some of the exercises that will help you to determine whether an opportunity is right for you. *Take action and exercise control in the areas where you can.* Practice the component behaviors, such as doing research and discussing your work, that produce the feeling that you are in control. Your newfound knowledge will give you confidence, and together these will make you a better job candidate.

As you apply the concepts presented in this book and practice the new behaviors you learn, you will find that your attitude about interviewing has changed. You will be less anxious and less nervous because you have taken steps to prepare properly for your interviews. You will feel (and be!) more in control of your job search because you are making choices that mean something to you, rather than reacting to the whims of the employment system. You will feel more powerful because you will be ready to offer value to anyone who interviews and hires you.

You will *do the job* in your interviews, just as you do your job every day: expertly and successfully.

CHAPTER 9

When It's Time to Call It a Day

This Job May Not Be for You

Your effectiveness in interviews will be greatly influenced by your ability to distinguish between the right job and the wrong jobs. That's not a typographical error: right J-O-B and wrong J-O-B-S. There are more wrong jobs for you out there than there are right jobs. And chances are that at least once in your life you will take the wrong job, just because it was offered to you. When you take a wrong job, you eventually will need to interview to find a right job. So before you jump into anything, think about this first: is the job you are considering the right job? Or is it just an easy job to get? Will you need a new job soon after you take this one?

Why bother fooling around, wasting your time always looking for another job? Decide now what the *right* job is, and go after it. When you pursue the right job, you will be more enthusiastic and you will interview better. You will be more likely to impress the employer and you will likely earn greater rewards. And, if your next job is the right job, you won't need to look for another one so soon.

How will you know that a job is the wrong job? To an unprepared candidate this can be very difficult to figure out. There are just too many factors outside the control of such a candidate, and any one of them may contribute to a sense that something is wrong. If you're unprepared, it's likely that *you* are the problem (see "Level of Preparedness" in chapter 5).

However, if you have followed the approach to job hunting that I have tried to teach you, you will know a job is wrong by thoughtfully applying the Four Questions. If you're prepared and you know you're ready to tackle the job, there aren't many reasons why a job may be wrong for you—but any single one of them can bring your interview experience to an unexpected close. Here are the most common issues:

1. The chemistry between you and the manager isn't right. There isn't much, if anything, you can do about this.

2. The job is different from what your research suggested it was, and you can't really do it. The only option here, other than bowing out gracefully, is to reconduct your research about the job right there in the interview. Find out what the manager needs. If he is willing, you may be able to come back for another interview, once you have prepared for it.

3. The job is broken. See chapter 4 for more about how to deal with this situation.

4. You can do the job, but decide you don't want it. (Your reasons may include learning that the growth path is not to your liking.) Bow out gracefully. In the next few sections of this chapter I will suggest some ways that you can capitalize on your interview anyway.

If you find yourself interviewing for the wrong job, no matter what the reason, end the interview. There's nothing wrong with saying, "It seems this job may not be right for me. You want to hire the best candidate to suit your needs, and I want to find the job that will make the best use of my skills. Perhaps we should end this interview." The interviewer will respect your integrity.

192

The meeting may just end at this point. Or, you can take advantage of the shift in the meeting's tone and pursue some of the ideas described below. The interviewer may ask you what kind of job you *are* looking for. Be ready to answer the question, because you may have found an employer who can help you. You also may have found the perfect new opportunity.

If the Shoe Doesn't Fit, Take a Barefoot Walk in the Grass

I have already pointed out that not every job will be "winnable" for you. You have to be qualified, and only you can decide if you're qualified to pursue a particular job. My point is that if you don't believe in your qualifications, you should not pursue jobs for which you are not suited. You should not try to bulldoze your way through the interview door.

Once you are in an interview, there is someone else who has to decide whether you're qualified for the job. What happens if you're pursuing *the right job,* and it turns out—during the interview—that it isn't right? What if the one other person who must decide whether you're qualified—the prospective employer—disagrees with you?

In every negotiation, there can be disagreement, and interviews are negotiations. This is the touchiest part of job hunting, and it is the part of the experience that can raise real self-doubt.

"You are not I; therein lies the irreparable calamity."* The fact that this quote comes from Vladimir Nabokov's novel *Invitation to a Beheading* is interesting, considering how some people feel about interviewing. But this coincidence aside, the point is that we can never be sure that someone else will think what we think, feel what we feel, or understand truth the way we do. Indeed, that is a calamity. But it is also what makes the world go round.

* Vladimir Nabokov, *Invitation to a Beheading* (New York: G. P. Putnam's Sons, 1959).

An interviewer may not believe that you are as qualified as you think you are. His decision may save you the agony of working at a job that isn't right for you. Then again, he might be wrong and lose an opportunity to hire an exceptional worker. Such a disagreement does not signify an unsuccessful interview. If it has been decided that you are not going to be hired, you and the interviewer can continue your discussion candidly, and your interview can still end successfully.

Relax, take your shoes off, and take a walk through the grass with the interviewer. You're in blue sky country, and you have nothing to lose by taking a chance. Let's look at how this meeting might still pay off.

Ask for Advice

Few of us are the greatest experts in our fields. There is always someone else whose knowledge or point of view may be of benefit to us. The person who interviews you can likely add something valuable to your understanding about yourself, your work, or your profession.

When at the end of an interview it is clear that you are not going to be hired, force yourself to shift your point of view. The interviewer is not your opponent, and he is certainly not your boss if he hasn't made you a job offer. He is not your judge and jury. He is someone trying to get a job done. The two of you have a lot in common. If you can convey this understanding to the interviewer, you will experience a shift in the conversation.

You're not getting the job. If you acknowledge that the interview is over, you can shift to another topic without making the interviewer feel you are still trying to convince him to hire you. Thank the interviewer for his time and observations. Tell him that although this isn't a match, you hope he found your discussion as useful as you did.

Ask him if he would be good enough to give you some blunt advice. Be prepared to listen carefully. *Don't talk anymore.* Let him talk. Start with the question "Can you give me some advice?" People love to give advice, and their advice might be very useful. Continue with one or more of the following questions, depending on how cooperative the interviewer is.

- What would you recommend I do to communicate better in an interview?
- I know that a person's skills and his attitude about his work determine how good a job he can do. What do you think I need to work on?
- Tell me *what I need to learn* to qualify for this job, if I were to apply for it again next year.
- If I were working for you, and you were firing me right now, what advice would you give me?
- Knowing what you know about me, if someone called you and asked you to give me a reference, no-holds-barred, what would you tell them?

You may be stunned at the advice you get. You might not like everything you hear, but think about it carefully. After the interview, whether you agree with the comments or not, *write them all down* as accurately as you can remember them. Put them away. Take your notes out in a few days and review them. What do you think? Is there anything about your job search that you should change?

Your Time Is Worth a Referral

Just because an interview does not lead to a job does not mean the interviewer does not know of a job for you. You have to judge whether the interviewer sees value in your skills. If you think he does, ask for a referral. More specifically, ask him one or more of the following questions:

- Does the interviewer think you might be able to help the company in some other department or division?
- Are there any other managers he would suggest you talk with?
- What are the company's growth plans? Is there a future place for you?
- When would new positions likely open up? With what managers?

If there is another department you are particularly interested in, this is the time to do some of the research you'll need. Ask about that department.

- What kinds of challenges is the department facing?
- What kinds of help does it need?
- Who manages it?
- Would the interviewer be kind enough to introduce you to the manager on your way out? (If it's not a good time for an introduction, don't fret. You now have a reference when you call that manager later; you were referred by the interviewer you just met. The first manager might even be willing to recommend you.)

No matter what business the interviewer is in, he or she likely knows other people in the same business. This kind of referral often carries the greatest weight.

- Can the interviewer recommend another good company that might benefit from your skills? Does he know a specific manager there?
- Is there someone he respects at another company who might be able to advise you?
- Which industry associations does the interviewer think are best? Is there a committee chairperson he knows who might be able to recommend opportunities elsewhere in the industry?

It's important for you to obtain *names* of people you can call on. It will help greatly if the manager gives you permission to use his name. Shake the interviewer's hand, and say, "Thank you. Your comments and your advice mean a lot to me. If there's ever anything I can do to help you or [the company], please call me." Look him straight in the eye when you say this. Leave your business card and ask for his.

Be a Capitalist

Being a capitalist means investing in an enterprise* with no guarantee of a return on your investment. Consider the popular credo "perform random acts of kindness." It means pretty much the same thing, except capitalism is not usually random.

When your interview is done, and it seems the job is not for you, or it seems you cannot convince the employer you're right for the job (even though you think you are), leave some good things behind with the idea of helping the employer, not yourself. For example:

1. Ask, "Is there anything I can do to help you or your company in any other way?"

2. If you know one, recommend another good candidate for the job.

3. If you can foster some other relationship that might benefit the company, do it. For instance, you might offer a sales lead.

4. After your interview, if you read an article the employer might find useful, send a copy along with your compliments.

---

*"Enterprise" can refer to a business, or to the act of interviewing. It's a very good word to use to describe your job search. Understanding the word will help you to see the broader significance of what you're trying to accomplish. Check a good dictionary for a detailed definition of the concept.

5. Don't send a typical thank-you note. Send an *acknowledgment*, saying you enjoyed the thought-provoking meeting you had with the employer. Offer any useful thoughts you might have about the job, but don't keep trying to win the job. Let it go.

There was a popular saying in the 1960s: "If you love something, let it go. If it was meant to be yours, it will come back." Trust me when I tell you that if you have met a fine person and established a professional rapport, sometime, somewhere, on some level, there is a good chance you will have an opportunity to work together. This kind of professional exchange is the foundation of a head-hunter's success—learn to make it part of your life.

Regroup

There is a tendency to rationalize not winning an offer after an interview. We all find excuses; we all cry "sour grapes." But that will hurt you in your job hunt, because it will make you less honest with yourself. If you have done all the work to prepare for an interview, you're selling yourself short if you make excuses rather than think hard about what happened in your interview.

At the heart of this book are two assumptions: you are honest with yourself, and you are dedicated to doing work that is worthwhile and valuable. We don't often get an opportunity to spend an hour or so talking with someone who has no preconceived notions about us. So take this stranger's—the interviewer's—observations and advice seriously. Use what you learn to add value to your work and to yourself.

Whether or not you agree with the outcome of your interview, you should pause to make some judgments about your capabilities, your skills, your motivation, and your ability to communicate. Learn from your experience *now* while it's fresh in your mind. Be honest with yourself.

Ideally, you were able to obtain some good feedback, even

advice, from the interviewer who did not hire you. Sit down and write out in detail his comments, as well as anything that prevented you from winning a job offer. Assume that whatever advice you were given is absolutely valid and accurate. Then list the changes you would have to make in yourself and your approach if you wanted to go after this job again.

An important way you can help yourself on your next interview is to do this analysis *now*. Go back to the notes you made during your preparation for the interview, and to the exercises you did in this book. Does your experience in this interview alter anything? Do you need to make revisions to your definition of your skills, abilities, or interests? Do you need to change the way you apply the Four Questions?

Of course, you may have left the interview convinced that you interviewed for the wrong job. It can happen, even with preparation. Nonetheless, the above exercise can help you prepare for your next venture. The conclusions you draw may affect the kinds of jobs you pursue, and they will undoubtedly affect how you handle your next employment meeting.

CHAPTER 10

Using the Headhunter's Strategy

Why Not Just Hire a Headhunter?

If your job search is not going well, you might decide to just hire a headhunter to help you. Why shouldn't you? One reason is that *you* must take responsibility for finding and winning your own new job. No one else will earn the kind of reward you will for finding that job. A career counselor may be willing to try, for a fee, but he does not have the skills and motivation of a headhunter. A head-hunter can do it, but his allegiance will never be to you; it is to his corporate clients.

The main reason, which many people do not understand, is that you *can't* hire a headhunter. Headhunters are paid by employers. A headhunter's long-term earnings depend on repeat business from companies whose needs and style he has gotten to know very well over time. Because you can't offer him the same kind of repeat business, the headhunter will not invest the same amount of time getting to know you.

You could search out a headhunter, but headhunters usually prefer to search out the right job candidates. They usually won't bother with you, unless you seem to be a match for a search they have been hired to conduct. You could just put your name out there to let headhunters know you're available. But that wouldn't guarantee you anything but exposure, and you don't want to be exposed as a job hunter to your own employer. Besides, hoping a headhunter will appear with the right job for you is the opposite of what I am trying to teach you to do: depend on your own skills to control your destiny.

So what's the big deal about using a headhunter's techniques to find a job, if a headhunter can't do it for you?

A headhunter *can* do it for you, using skills that no one else has. But, it's not what he does for a living. A headhunter is paid by his client to find the right person for a job. He is not paid to find the right job for you. The headhunter is very good at one thing that you must be able to do for yourself: identify the missing piece that fits into the puzzle.

In the headhunter's puzzle, a specific job is missing a critical piece: the right worker. In your puzzle, a worker with specific skills is missing a critical piece: the right job. The headhunter knows exactly how to proceed to solve the puzzle *efficiently and accurately*. When he finds the right candidate for his puzzle (the open job he's been hired to fill) the headhunter will apply all his skills and cunning to help that candidate win the job.

To solve your own puzzle, you can use the same strategy and techniques the headhunter uses. But, don't count on him to do it for you. Getting a headhunter's attention is like playing the lottery: if your number comes up, you win, and the reward is just as real as if you earned it yourself. You were in the right place at the right time. Enjoy it! But understand that the person drawing the numbers isn't trying to pick your number when he reaches into the spinning basket of tickets.

If a headhunter calls you, remember that opportunity sometimes does knock, and you must be ready. If the job happens to be one you want, you're still competing with other candidates. The difference is, you're competing with other candidates the headhunter is preparing for the same interview you're going on. You still have to take control, and use all the resources at your disposal to present yourself as the best candidate to both the headhunter and the employer who's paying his fee.

A headhunter can help you only if you fit the job he's being paid to fill. However, his approach can help you with any job you want to win, if you apply the approach yourself.

Make the Headhunter's Strategy Yours

This book started with the claim that headhunters know something other people don't know about job hunting. We have discussed that special knowledge at length. Now we're going to close by reviewing the most important concepts that headhunters apply to their work, and by briefly recapping how to apply these concepts to your job search.

A good headhunter has a simple view of the world: "I will place as many workers in the right jobs as quickly as I can, keeping my clients satisfied so that they will pay me to place more." Your mission is to find your own job, to do it quickly and intelligently, and to make it the right job.

A headhunter's goal is to earn as many fees as possible. To accomplish that, he has to get the right candidate in front of the right manager just when the manager needs to hire him. The headhunter's long-term goal is to make sure that the match works out to everyone's satisfaction. His methods work; if they didn't, he would not earn a living. Your mission is exactly the same, but you don't have to do it as often. You won't earn a fee, but you will earn a good job.

The headhunter's strategy is pragmatic. It ignores the traditional rules of the employment industry. It focuses on the job, the worker, and the match. Techniques are used flexibly, to match the job with the right worker. Your strategy should be exactly the same.

This view of the world can help you find your next good job. Let's translate the headhunter's strategy into a few simple instructions that can work for you.

1. Go after jobs that you know are definitely right for you.

Headhunters don't waste their time with bad matches. They invest their time in the right ones. This is why employers rely on headhunters. Many job hunters will scan the ads and make a list of the jobs that seem suited to them. Their research ends right there. Résumés are mailed out without further thought. If one of these mailings results in a call, the eager job hunter drops everything and rushes to the interview.

The job hunter gets on an emotional roller coaster. Having gotten this interview without first answering the Four Questions about the job, he is nonetheless elated at being invited to interview. In his elation, he convinces himself that what has been handed to him is what he wants. Unprepared, he fails to win an offer. He can't figure out why he was turned down. Consequently, he develops a case of poor self-esteem that adversely affects the rest of his job hunt. If the job hunter gets an offer for one of these jobs, he's impressed with his "success" and accepts it, only to find himself miserable a few months into the wrong job.

Apply the Four Questions to analyze every job opportunity. Select and prepare only for one that is right for you. Decide whether you will shine in the interview. Is it a job you could do better than almost anyone else? Can you prove it to the employer by doing the job during the interview? Would the employer earn greater profits if he hired you? Once you are hired and on the job, will you feel you have achieved your goal?

---

2. Go after real jobs.

Personnel departments, other employees, employment agencies, and want ads are notoriously wrong about what jobs are really open in a company. Headhunters work only with the source of the job.

If you've heard about an attractive job, remember that's just *a lead*. Find out who the manager is and get your information directly from the source: the manager who's doing the hiring.

If you want to be strung along without any indication that a company really intends to hire you, keep mailing your résumé to personnel departments and interview only with personnel representatives. Their job is to collect and file as many people as they can, in anticipation of future hiring. Their job is also to screen people out. Do you want a first-year personnel jockey deciding you're not qualified for a technical job that he doesn't really understand?

Ads can also be dangerous blind alleys. Do you have any idea where your résumé winds up when you respond to an ad? Especially a "blind ad" that doesn't name the employer? Too often, it winds up in résumé jail—a filing cabinet—and *you never even know it.* Good luck trying to arrange bail. You might as well buy a lottery ticket.

Newspapers and employers engage in yet another practice that conspires to waste more of your time. In consideration for running a continuous want ad (for several weeks or months), a publication will guarantee a special low ad rate to an advertiser. When this employer has no jobs to advertise, he must run an ad anyway to keep the discount. The ad is called a "composite." A little bit of this job, a little bit of that one. "Let's see who responds." There is no real job for you. You submit your résumé; it goes to jail.

3. Do all the necessary preparation before the interview.

Do everything a headhunter would do: research the industry, the company, the interviewer, the job, the department where the job lives. Prepare the way, grease the skids.

> Read, study, do research. Learn everything you can about the company, the job, and the people. Get to know the secretary. Get to know the manager. Talk to vendors. Talk to customers. Talk to competitors. Talk to other employees. Talk to other departments. Only go on the interview if you know your chances of winning an offer have been maximized ahead of time.

4. Know beforehand whether the manager will be impressed with you.

Headhunters send only the best, most qualified, most motivated, most prepared candidates to meet a client. That's why they command the fees they do. Their job is to send in the right candidate *and they do their job*. Shouldn't you be at least as good a candidate as the candidate a headhunter sends in?

> Never go on an interview unless you're convinced you will make the manager say "Wow!"

Maybe you won't *succeed* in impressing him, but shouldn't you *prepare* to do just that? Otherwise, why are you wasting your time and his time?

5. Make sure the employer knows you can do the job.

I will go right on repeating this. If you just got your hands on this book and somehow your eyes fell on this paragraph before you've read anything else, I should tell you right now that this is what *Ask the Headhunter* is all about.

> Do the job in the interview.

6. Ask for the interviewer's opinion.

An employer has made a decision about you before you're out the door, but he usually won't tell you. A good headhunter is on the phone talking to the employer about the outcome of an interview before his candidate has left the employer's building.

> At the end of your meeting, ask the interviewer what he thinks of you, and whether he is convinced you can do the job.

If an interviewer won't tell you when you ask, explain to him that you were glad to invest your time in this meeting to help him evaluate your ability to do the job. Now you would like the courtesy of his honest opinion. If he still can't, or won't, answer you then either he is not the one doing the hiring or he doesn't know how to politely turn you down to your face. The bottom line is, this person is not going to hire you.

7. Ask the interviewer if he thinks you are a viable candidate.

If the interviewer gave you his opinion of you, get more specific with this question:

> Do you believe I can do the job the way you want it done and help you to make your business more profitable?

You can bet a headhunter asks the employer this question about every candidate he submits. Getting the employer to *say* it is a powerful way to make him *act* on it.

8. Make sure the employer knows you want the job.

Would you seriously consider an offer to do this job? (Forget about the money at this point—just focus on the job and the work. You can negotiate for money later.) Yes? Then go for the gold—especially if you sense that the employer is impressed with you. You owe it to both yourself and the employer to tell him in no uncertain terms that you want the job before you leave the interview. You may be the only candidate who comes out and says it.

> Look the employer right in the eye, without a trace of a smile on your face, and say, "I hope I have convinced you that I can do this job, and do it well. I would enjoy working on your team. I want this job."

This is the most important claim a headhunter makes to a company on behalf of any candidate he sends in for an interview.

9. Close the deal.

If he's ready to hire you and tells you so, don't panic. You don't have to sign a contract just yet. Thank him, and tell him you think your meeting was a success and that you're excited about doing the job. Tell him you're looking forward to receiving a written offer that includes all the details of your employment agreement. How soon can he get it to you? You'll have an answer for him three days (or a week, or whatever you think is reasonable) after you receive the written offer.

After you leave his office, start making some notes about what you need to do next to help you decide whether you're going to accept this offer. Start thinking about whether you'd really be happy doing this job at this company for this manager, if the terms are (or can be negotiated) to your liking.

As soon as you receive the written offer, review it carefully. What information do you still need? Who else at the company do you need to meet? Do any aspects of the offer still need to be negotiated? That's exactly what a headhunter considers on behalf of his candidate, except he's also calculating his fee.

The same day you receive the written offer, call the employer. *Talk directly with him,* not with anyone else representing him. Confirm that you just received the offer. He may be surprised it took so long. His personnel jockeys probably wrote it up and mailed it, and they probably took a lot longer than he (or you) expected.* Tell

*I've had clients call me, anxiously wondering why a candidate has not responded to their offer—and I've had to tell them their human resources department has not yet *sent* the written offer.

him again that you're pleased he made you an offer. Since your meeting, you've found there are a few things you would like to discuss with him in person. Could he arrange for you to meet with him, and with some of the other people on his team, in the next few days? Review "The Power of the Offer" in chapter 6 and use it to help you negotiate the deal you want.

If it turns out that this job offer is not right for you, and it can't be negotiated into a form you want, gracefully thank the employer and explain that although the job is what you were looking for, the terms and conditions are not. Express your regrets that the two of you could not reach a mutually acceptable agreement. Go on to a new, and hopefully better opportunity.

Your search has come to an end if this job offer is what you want. Congratulations! When you start your new job, apply the same concepts to *doing your work* that you applied toward finding it. Stop periodically and ask the Four Questions about your work. *Do the job*, and you will find that new doors will always open to you, in your own company and in others.

APPENDIX: A PICTURE OF THE NEW INTERVIEW CONCEPTS

This is a graphical representation of the main steps to finding the right new job. Refer to the text for detailed discussion about each step and how to accomplish it.

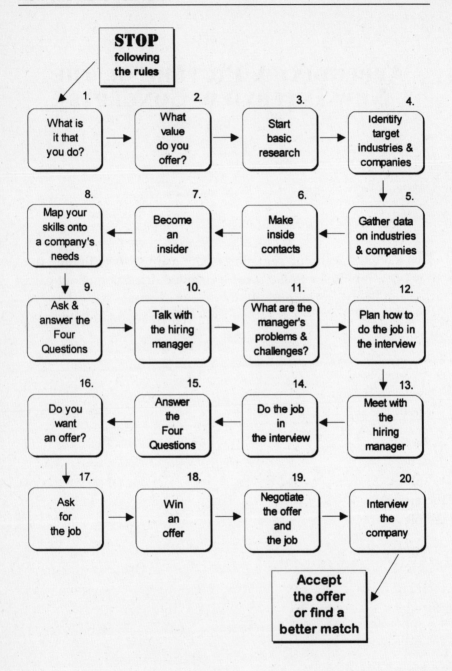

RECOMMENDED READING

The great majority of a person's day is spent working. It is therefore important to have a well-thought-out philosophy about your work, and it should mesh with your attitudes and beliefs about life, family, money, and change. These books have given me useful insights into all of these topics. I hope you find them enjoyable and helpful.

Atlas Shrugged by Ayn Rand (Signet, 1992).
This is a classic mystery about life, work, love, and integrity. It inspired me to finally write *Ask the Headhunter*.

Influence: The Psychology of Persuasion by Robert Cialdini (Quill, 1993).
This book offers a close, practical look at how and why people agree to things in their personal and work lives. It thoroughly describes the mechanisms of influence. It will help you understand how other people influence your life, and how you influence theirs.

Moneylove by Jerry Gillies (Warner Books, 1985).
This is the best book I've ever read about how to eliminate negative thinking by changing your behavior. The focus is on how people's attitudes about money can limit their search for success. Don't let the title fool you: the book is about how to build a healthy attitude about life.

Wealth and Poverty by George Gilder (ICS Press, 1993).
An illuminating, thoughtful book about why people live and work

together, and why some are more successful than others. A good companion to *Moneylove.*

The Assertive Woman, third edition, by Nancy K. Austin and Stanlee Phelps (Impact Publishing, 1997).
No woman or man should be without this book. It will teach you how to turn your life into action.

Conceptual Blockbusting: A Guide to Better Ideas by James Adams (Addison-Wesley, 1990).
This is an eye-opening, fun guide to overcoming mental blocks and putting your skills to work to solve problems.

Social Learning Theory by Albert Bandura (Prentice-Hall, 1977).
This is an overview of important psychological research about how people's behavior and thought processes combine to produce learning and change. Not an easy read, but worth the investment.

The Pursuit of WOW by Tom Peters (Vintage Books, 1994).
A great "kick in the mind," Tom's list of idea-provoking thoughts and stories on the business of work will have you charging out the door to do something smart.

About the Author

Nick Corcodilos earned his credentials as a headhunter in California's Silicon Valley. He has helped executives, middle managers, engineers, and other professionals obtain positions in companies such as Xerox, IBM, General Electric, Hewlett-Packard, Honeywell, and Bell Aerospace. As a sales executive and a management consultant he has worked with companies of all sizes, as well as with government agencies and academic institutions.

Today Corcodilos's firm, North Bridge Group, helps companies develop more effective strategies for selecting, interviewing, and hiring the right workers. Using the concepts in this book, Nick also provides an alternative to traditional outplacement to Fortune 500 companies, helping "downsized" workers win the right new jobs either internally or externally. His job-search coaching is available on a private basis to individual clients.

Nick Corcodilos is a popular speaker both in person and online. His *Ask the Headhunter* forum appears on America Online at keyword [headhunter] and on the internet at [http://www.asktheheadhunter.com]. Hosted by The Motley Fool, *Ask the Headhunter* has helped thousands of job hunters and employers tackle the challenge of matching the right person with the right job.

Nick Corcodilos holds bachelor's and master's degrees in cognitive psychology from Rutgers College and Stanford University. His work has been featured in publications such as Tom Peters's *On Achieving Excellence* and *Fast Forward, Working Woman* magazine, the

His work has been featured in publications such as Tom Peters's *On Achieving Excellence* and *Fast Forward, Working Woman* magazine, the *National Business Employment Weekly, Electronic Engineering Times,* Peter Drucker's *Leader to Leader, Sales & Marketing Management* magazine, *Smart Workplace Practices, Bottom Line Business* and Merrill Lynch's *Business Insights.*

Nick Corcodilos can be reached via E-mail at North Bridge Group at NBGroup@aol.com

TONE 1661   1st Proof   2 Roughs   5-22-97
Penguin   Ask the Headhunter — 0-452-27801-5   News Gothic   Gal. 2

℗ **PLUME**

WORDS TO THE CAREER-WISE

☐ **THE AFRICAN AMERICAN NETWORK** *Get Connected to More Than 5,000 Prominent People and Organizations in the African American Community* **by Crawford B. Bunkley.** This essential volume contains an A-to-Z listing of the names of more than 5,000 individuals and organizations with important connections in fields such as sports, politics and the arts. Also included are the names and addresses of the most important civil rights associations, education organizations, religious organizations, trade associations, and bookstores and publishers.   (274931—$14.95)

☐ **MOVING ON** *How to Make the Transition from College to the Real World* **by Jessica Fein.** Now that you hold a degree, no one is holding your hand anymore. How will you find a job? Or pay rent? Will you be happy with your new life? This lively, upbeat guide filled with colorful anecdotes from veterans of the big move will help you avoid the pitfalls of real life. Survive on your own like a real adult—now that your are one!   (276039—$11.95)

☐ **THE ULTIMATE CREDIT HANDBOOK** *How to Double Your Credit, Cut Your Debt, and Have a Lifetime of Great Credit* **by Gerri Detweiler.** *Revised and Updated!* The definitive resource on credit—how to get it, how to keep it, how to manage it, how to get more of it for less, and how to profit from it. Credit can be a blessing or a curse. The choice is yours—and now the tools that make the difference are in your hands.   (277124—$12.95)

Prices slightly higher in Canada.

Visa and Mastercard holders can order Plume, Meridian, and Dutton books by calling
1-800-253-6476.
They are also available at your local bookstore. Allow 4-6 weeks for delivery.
This offer is subject to change without notice.